MW00460341

Tales from Country Music

Gerry Wood

Sports Publishing L.L.C.
www.SportsPublishingLLC.com

© 2003 Gerry Wood
All Rights Reserved.

Director of production: Susan M. Moyer
Project manager: Greg Hickman
Developmental editor: Erin Linden-Levy
Copy editor: Cynthia L. McNew
Dust jacket design: Kerri Baker

ISBN: 1-58261-651-1

Printed in the United States.

SPORTS PUBLISHING L.L.C.
www.SportsPublishingLLC.com

Dedication

My co-authors have been by my side for a dozen years, honoring me with total devotion, unaffected affection, hilarious shenanigans, and priceless brown/white/black fur for my fingers to luxuriate in when I seek total peace and serenity. As I write, they gather close for encouragement and support, never knowing that I worship them more than they worship me, if that is at all possible.

Captain and Calhoun enjoyed the high life of Key West, stars in their own right as tourists adventuring past our home, East of Ernest, snapped photos of the Southernmost Beagles, posing proud and protective on the front porch. Their favorite guest was Jerry Jeff Walker, who sang his hit "Mr. Bojangles" for them. The Beagle Brothers didn't like the line about "the dog up and died," but I understand the message of the lyric, "after 20 years he still grieves."

Later, they moved to Nashville, dragging me along with them, where they cavorted with the dog-loving country music stars. Tammy Wynette's tiny pet Killer traveled with her—a dog's life aboard a luxury tour bus. Wynonna's menagerie keeps expanding. Tom T. and Dixie Hall once raised more than 50 Bassett hounds. K. T. Oslin's dog loved the daily walks in New York City's Central Park. When K.T. learned her dog was dying and was too weak for the walk, she hired a limousine, rolled down the windows and took her furry friend on a final trip through the park in style.

Sadly, during the writing of this book, Captain died. He was such a special spirit, a nourishing healer who helped rescue a young woman from a breakdown, attached himself to a shy neighbor kid whom I later learned had been sexually abused, worried himself silly about me, and found Heaven on earth any time he could snooze with his chin on my lap or Calhoun's back. Because of Captain's perpetual motion tail, his momma Carol tagged him The Wags. She described the impact of our loss by saying, "I'm

The Beagle Brothers—Captain, left, and Calhoun, right.
(Photo courtesy of Gerry Wood)

doing okay except I've got this big vacant spot inside me where Captain used to be."

Calhoun continues his heartbreakingly futile search for his missing brother, and then, with his ears pinned back, his big beagle eyes stare at me, pleading and confused. Knowing that I've always made everything right for him, Calhoun can't understand why I'm unable to do that one more time and bring back his brother. I try to explain it to him until I realize that I don't understand death either. Then I just tell him that Captain would want us to carry on, and that's what we are doing. As author James W. Hall observes, "Though the pain of their loss is great, the loss of their joy-giving would be even more difficult."

In remembrance of our late and great co-author, Calhoun and I dedicate this book to Captain. Thanks, Wags. Like I've always said, you and Calhoun are the best beagles in the business. We love you and miss you.

Calhoun and Gerry Wood
Nashville, Tennessee
2003

Acknowledgments

Beyond the Beagle Brothers, this book is dedicated to the Harnisches of the Hamptons, where I give thanks when spending Thanksgiving. For Louise Harnisch, the Grand Duchess of the Hamptons, thanks for making me family. For Bill Harnisch, your scorched friend is happy to serve as your heat shield any time you need it. For Ruth Ann Harnisch, here's hoping that someday I'll be more worth than I'm trouble. Your friendship through the decades deserves that.

Sorry, George Strait, but none of my exes live in Texas. Everlasting love, respect and appreciation go to my ex-wife Ellen in Nashville and my ex-fiancé Carol in Key West. Hmmm, what's wrong with this picture?

My heartfelt appreciation to Naomi Judd for contributing her brilliant foreword. She's the beautiful incarnation of what a country music star should embody in talent, intelligence and compassion. Naomi, Wynonna and Ashley Judd not only have the best taste in basketball teams—the University of Kentucky Wildcats—they share a family tradition of remarkable performances on record, on the stage, on television and on the silver screen.

Another honor comes from one of my heroes, Garrison Keillor, allowing the inclusion of his masterful eulogy for Chet Atkins—the centerpiece of Chet's memorial service. Garrison's profound and eloquent tribute raised the craft of writing and potential of verbal communication several notches beyond all pretenders to his throne. They say that a picture is worth a thousand words, but Keillor's words about Chet are worth a thousand pictures.

Kudos to some special family members—Judi and Graham Wood, Linda Ford, Stephanie Ford, Calhoun Wood and my heaven-dispatched parents Gladys and Albert Wood—now dogsitting, and loving it, with Joe Roach and Captain Wood.

I've worked with editors at Random House and Simon & Schuster, but nobody tops Erin Linden-Levy of Sports Publishing L.L.C., with her skillful advice and inspiring support. Thanks to Paul Zamek for guiding this project into my corner and to Bob Snodgrass for pushing it into reality.

Good friends will be with you through thick and thin. Great friends will be with you through *thin* and thin. Some of my great friends: Charlie Monk, Tom Webb, Joe Sweat, Chuck Neese, Dave Springer, Stella Parton, Ed Morris, Susan Niles, Merle Kilgore, Caroline Davis, Bob Beckham, Rhonda Smith, Walter Sill, Lorian Hemingway, Jeff Baker, Shannon Parks-Denton, Harry Warner, Debbie Holley, Bucci Brother Terry Brown, Charlie Neese, Pegg Vanek, Tom Jernigan and Roxane Robinson, Charlie and Lorna Jean Walker, Tom T. and Dixie Hall, and the world's greatest photographer—Raeanne Rubenstein, my Manhattan hillbilly friend forever. Our Raeanne/Gerry photographer/writer team routinely turns the blasé into the bizarre. From heartbreak at Bobbie Cryner's house to fake eggs in George "Goober" Lindsey's kitchen, we've enjoyed and/or suffered it all.

Finally, a double Irish toast to the dear departed Ed Shea, my boss at the American Society of Composers, Authors and Publishers. A whiz at remembering birthdays, Ed was a disaster when recalling names. After I had worked with Shea for five years, he once called me Bob Woods. Our assistant director Charlie Monk fared worse when Ed introduced him as Rufus Monk. One morning Shea told me he had seen Roger Miller perform on television the night before. "Are you *sure* it was Roger Miller?" I asked. "I'm positive!" Ed answered with conviction. "He was on the *Jimmy Carson Show.*"

And now…on with the *Jimmy Carson Show*!

Contents

Introduction

Confessions of a Country Junkie

Yes, Father, I have come to confess my sins. I've got a biggie for you. Is this confessional booth soundproof? Might be a *National Enquirer* reporter eavesdropping, ready to blow my credibility to smithereens if he hears what I'm about to tell you. There's a shady guy lingering at the front of the church, washing his hands in the holy water. He might have the holiest hands in the land, but I don't believe he's one of us.

"Could you please cut to the chase, my son? I'm already late for a stockholders' meeting. Our CEO, Martha Stewart, is supposed to make a personal appearance. We've got some questions for her."

Oh, I'm sorry, Father, please forgive me. Forgive Martha Stewart, too, while you're at it. Are you taking your mobile confessional booth with you?

"No, it's in the shop for repairs. Blew a gasket when I took it to Washington, D.C. last week for a joint session of Congress. Now, proceed."

Yes, Father. I have worked most of my life in the country music business, and now I'm writing a book about it.

"That's not a mortal sin. A little borderline, perhaps, but I can get you off on that one."

Thank you. But that's not what I want to confess. It's something much more serious.

"This is not the new Fox TV reality show, *Guess My Sin*. What is the transgression?"

Father, here it is: I grew up hating country music.

"Could you repeat that? I don't think I heard you correctly."

I grew up hating country music. I was the only Kentuckian who hated bluegrass music and country music.

"My God, son! Are you serious?"

Yes, Father, I told you this was a big-time blunder.

"We're talking a lot of Hail Marys here, and enough penance to push Hank Williams through the pearly gates with Spade Cooley not far behind. Were there any mitigating circumstances for this aberration?"

Yes. It wasn't my fault. It was Jimmy Lambert's fault.

"Well, get him in here, too. Is he a Christian?"

No, he's a Presbyterian. But he's the one who did it. He's responsible for my early dislike of country music. Father, what's that beeping noise?

"Sorry, my son—the cell phone. Hang on. Oh, hello, Slick. Tell them I'll be late. I've got an emergency here. Some sinner who hates country music and is writing a book for country music lovers. This has gone beyond mortal. Later. Bye."

Father, let me explain. When I was a teenager in Henderson, Kentucky, I used to spend Saturday nights with Jimmy Lambert, one of my best friends. The Lamberts lived in this big hilltop home, and Jimmy had the entire second floor bedroom. He loved fresh air, which is not a bad trait, except he left all the windows wide open, even in the middle of winter during the zero degree days. *That* is a bad trait. Jimmy slept in his bed and I slept in mine, which was equipped only with a single sheet to cover myself. Father, I was freezing my a—, forgive me, freezing my rear end off. Between the beds was a desk where Jimmy kept his pet turtle in a glass jar. We woke up one morning and the water in the jar was frozen over. Poor turtle. Poor me. Looking back, I believe Jimmy was experimenting with the first cryogenic freezing of bodies. He might have been ahead of his time, but both of us lost brain cells in the process. While I shivered under the sheet, he would turn on the radio full-blast, the volume reaching 11 on a scale of one to 10. The announcer's voice boomed, "This is WCKY, Cincinnati One, Ohio." And then I knew I was in for a long night of upper-register sounds that had the dogs howling for miles away. Later in life I learned that I was listening to Hank Williams and Ernest Tubb and Bill Monroe and Roy Acuff—

performers whom I grew to admire—but back then, it was like a vision of Hell if Satan had turned the heat off. Father, I don't mean to carry on.

"That's okay, my son, I am finding this quite illuminating. I dread being chilly myself."

Jimmy personified Barbara Mandrell's number one song, "I Was Country When Country Wasn't Cool." Except *he* was country and I wasn't cool. I was *cold*. The bitter weather and country hits got all tangled up and confused in the tiny portion of my brain that wasn't frozen solid.

"Have you repented?"

Yes, Father, I told Jimmy I was sorry that he turned me against country music, but that I grew out of that stage and now love it. Although, honestly, I was still having some problems with bluegrass music until I heard Rhonda Vincent. But Jimmy was impressed that I'm writing a book on some of my favorite country stars.

"You are forgiven. You'll be interviewing these stars?"

Yes, Father.

"You can call me Bob."

Yes, Bob.

"Could you do me a favor since you've made me late for my meeting?"

Sure, Father Bob.

"Any chance you could get me an autographed photo of Shania Twain?"

It's summer, 2003, in Nashville and I am amazed how someone who grew up with a dislike for country music now loves it so much. The answer comes from both sides of the stage: the fans and the artists.

As chronicled in the anecdotes that follow, the world's biggest country music festival, Fan Fair, annually tests the fidelity and survival power of entertainers and their audience. Formerly held at the Tennessee State Fairgrounds, the event has moved to downtown Nashville—and more changes are on the way.

The 2004 version is expected to forgo the Fan Fair name in favor of a new moniker—the Country Music Association Music Festival. According to CMA officials, the 33rd annual presentation also will expand into additional music genres. Attendees at the 2003 Fan Fair offered mixed opinions of the changes, putting the CMA on the defensive. Many questioned why the Fan Fair name is being dropped and whether pop or rock acts might elbow out some of their country favorites.

It's doubtful that the stages of Fan Fair, whoops, the Country Music Association Music Festival, will ever host the likes of Marilyn Manson, Ozzy Osbourne, Eminem, Snoop Dog or Lil Jon & the East Side Boys. But the Charlie Daniels Jams and Willie Nelson's Farm Aid concerts—with acts ranging from Hootie & the Blowfish to David Allan Coe—prove that country, pop and rock acts can please fans from all camps. Non-country acts who might score with Festival fans include Bruce Springsteen, John Prine, Lionel Richie, James Taylor, Jackson Browne, Arlo Guthrie, Celine Dion, Delbert McClinton, Neil Young, John Hiatt and Amy Grant. Stay tuned for the latest details.

The funeral service for June Carter Cash (1929-2003) demonstrated once again the conscience and character of the Grammy-winning singer-writer-actress. Daughter of Mother Maybelle Carter, June loved fresh flowers. For that reason, the family added a poignant twist to the traditional request of "In lieu of flowers, please send donations to...." For June, the message was changed to: "In lieu of donations, please send flowers."

Located near the lakeside home she lived in and loved in with her husband Johnny Cash, the church sanctuary looked like the Tennessee Botanical Gardens as Rosanne Cash, Johnny's daughter, saluted her stepmother. "She did not give birth to me," Rosanne said, wiping away tears, "but she helped me give birth to my future."

Rosanne also provided a telling insight into the personality of June, the Carter Family Renaissance woman who moved with equal grace whether visiting friends in rugged mountain cabins or in the majesty and power of the White House. She described walking into the Cash's kitchen one day while June was engaged in an animated phone call, offering advice and encouragement to the person on the other end of the line. The conversation lasted about twenty minutes. When June finally said goodbye and hung up, Rosanne asked her what friend she was talking to. Answered June: "Well, honey, I don't know who it was—it was a wrong number."

The fortunate person who mistakenly ended up talking to June Carter Cash certainly had dialed the right wrong number.

Despite my frigid introduction to the world of country music, I have enjoyed three wonderful decades covering these internationally known entertainers. The adventures have taken me snorkeling with members of Rascal Flatts in the Cayman Islands, on a wild California plane trip with Hank Williams, Jr., aboard the tour buses of Diamond Rio, Lonestar, the Oak Ridge Boys and Garth Brooks and into the homes of such stars as Barbara Mandrell, Kenny Rogers, Earl Scruggs, Deborah Allen, George Jones, Aaron Tippin, Skeeter Davis, Tanya Tucker, Joe Diffie, Randy Travis, Trace Adkins, Sammy Kershaw, Mark Chesnutt and Tracy Byrd.

Meanwhile the Kentucky boyhood friend who introduced me to cryogenic country music moved to Nag's Head, North Carolina, where he thawed out enough to write songs—country songs, of course. Jimmy Lambert celebrated July 4, 2003, with the news that two of the most revered legends in country music history, Willie Nelson and Ray Price, had just released a critically acclaimed duet version of his ballad "Run That By Me One More Time."

The biggest problem in creating this book wasn't surviving Jimmy's introduction to country music or coming up with enough yarns; it was selecting which ones to include. There are so many more. Like the night Mark Chesnutt took me to a wet T-shirt contest at a Corpus Christi, Texas, nightclub. Or when a boozing Faron Young frantically investigated all of Johnny Cash's closets and cabinets, complaining, "I know Johnny's got the hooch in here somewhere!" Or the time that a beautiful singer lit up marijuana in my ASCAP office just as a law officer arrived at the door to sell me a ticket to the Policeman's Ball. I yanked it out of her mouth and hid it, admonishing, "What's a joint like this doing in a girl like you?" Needless to say, I bought a bunch of tickets to the Policeman's Ball, which—also needless to say—neither of us attended.

And, of course, there are some stories I will never tell. At least until the statute of limitations expires.

Gerry Wood

Foreword
by
Naomi Judd

On May 8, 1987, I sent a letter to Gerry Wood, then the Nashville and Southern region bureau chief of *Billboard* magazine. He had written one of his "Nashville Scene" columns on the Academy of Country Music Awards in Los Angeles, and he said some really positive things about Wynonna and me and our participation on the show.

He also touched on a topic that caused me to write the letter—respect. Respect for those who devote their energies and talents to raising the profile and popularity of country music to the levels enjoyed by other forms of music. And respect for country music itself. Here's what I wrote in that letter, and I stand by it today:

Dear Gerry:

Just a quick "thank you" for your Nashville Scene article in the April 25ᵗʰ issue. Of course, we're glad you thought the Academy of Country Music show was memorable, but more important to Wynonna and me, you took that extra step to say that the show "won the respect of the country music industry from California to Nashville." Honestly, Gerry, that is a big part of what we're doing out here—working on winning that respect. I think there's some serious company in that attempt.

It's more than hype and blowing whistles about each other in the country music community. The real business is putting our collective feet on the same soil as everyone else in the whole entertainment field. Country music comes from a tradition as deep as our Scotch-Irish roots and as broad as the melting pot of American society. We demand that respect.

Again, thanks.

A Faithful Reader,

Naomi Judd

Naomi Judd
(Photo courtesy of Naomi Judd)

Since I wrote that letter some 16 years ago, many of my hopes and dreams about the future of country music have been realized. Wynonna and I have learned firsthand that our music has earned not only the respect, but also the admiration of entertainers in other genres of music and show business. From radio airplay, to concerts, to network and cable television, to media coverage that rivals any other style of music, country music has reached the top.

Some of the media attention has been helpful, and some has hurt, especially when the tabloids targeted our private lives. It seems that Wynonna, Ashley and I have become poster children for selling their publications. But Gerry Wood has been covering us accurately and with respect ever since we signed with RCA Records in 1983 when he ran *Billboard* in New York City, and later when he wrote for *People* and *Country Weekly* and appeared on The Nashville Network.

As Wynonna puts it, "He's the one who gets it right."

I'm not sure he got it all the way right when he called the Judds "the most dysfunctional family in country music" as he was interviewed on A&E's award-winning *Biography* show on The Judds. I sent Gerry a card that said, "Thanks for taking part in the show and for your free psychological evaluation of our family." And then Wynonna reminded me that the Judds are the family that puts the "fun" in "dysfunctional."

Gerry has been in the front row for some of the milestone events in our show business lives. He was there when RCA introduced this new unknown duo to radio and media 20 years ago. He was there a year later when we won our first Country Music Association award. He was there when we were honored to perform at a benefit concert at Washington's Constitution Hall in tribute to Vietnam veterans on the fifth anniversary of the Vietnam Veterans Memorial. The event featured Bob Hope, Alabama and The Judds. Here's what Gerry wrote about the show in *Billboard*:

"The concert was electric. The Judds have never been better. When Wynonna Judd tried to express her feelings about the importance of this performance, emotion overcame her. Naomi clasped her daughter's shoulder in support, and the message was delivered without words. Both The Judds and Alabama were called back for encores. This was a special show, a special night."

He's been there in the best of times and the worst of times. When chronic hepatitis forced me to end our career as The Judds in 1991, it was one of the most devastating emotional times of my life. During that press conference, I looked around at the faces of friends and those who had followed our career that was now ending. Gerry, a journalist who is supposed to be hard-nosed and thick-skinned, looked at me, and he was fighting back tears. And he was there during the good times again, as I conquered my illness and set back out on the road with Wynonna once again. And there he was during our millennium concert in Phoenix, sitting there with his lady friend Chris Yerby and her mother June—just the perfect family way to launch the year of 2000 and the new millennium ahead.

Country music, based on a storyteller tradition through tales set to music, offers a rich repertoire of anecdotes concerning the lives and loves of those who have made this style so successful. Some are funny, some are tragic, some are a little bit crazy, and others are philosophical and inspiring. I'm so happy that one chapter in this book is devoted to our own tales about one of our all-time favorite performers and what she meant to us professionally and personally—Tammy Wynette.

In this day of yellow (checkbook) journalism, Gerry stands head and shoulders above the rest. His experience and knowledge are unparalleled. And I enjoy his personality so much that I count him as a friend. Whether it's tales in tribute to Tammy, Gerry's fascinating two-day trip across Texas with Willie Nelson, or a journey with Patty Loveless on the Santa Train's holiday gift-giving run through the edge of Kentucky—the state we're all from—Gerry Wood has the tales. And he's here to tell them.

Chapter 1

Survival of the Finest

"Are you someone?" Fans ask unknown artists that debilitating question with a naïve cruelty. This nervous country singer was such a stranger during Fan Fair 1976 that she wore a "Hello-My-Name-Is" sticker on her dress, proclaiming that she really *was* someone.

That sticker carried the name Reba McEntire. Yes, she was someone who would become a much more well known someone in a few years.

She sat patiently in the Mercury Records booth with a sign behind her announcing that Reba McEntire was ready to sign autographs, pose for photos, chat, hug, kiss, whatever. But the fans ignored Reba, racing past her lonely little table to chase after Loretta Lynn, Charley Pride, Conway Twitty and other superstars.

Heartbroken and embarrassed, Reba shared the icy isolation with her consoling mother, who joined her in the tiny booth. McEntire's records weren't exactly setting the world on fire—her first three singles reached no higher than

Reba McEntire shows Gerry Wood her Stringtown,
Oklahoma, ranch for a People *magazine story.*
(Photo courtesy of Gerry Wood)

number 86 on *Billboard's* country chart. But she was a new
artist on a major label, and it seemed like at least one fan in
the thousands who flocked to Fan Fair would come up and
ask for an autograph.

Finally, after what seemed an eternity to Reba, a middle-
aged couple cautiously approached the thin, pale, redhead
from Oklahoma. Reba was ready for visitors—she was armed
with a Sharpie pen and a large stack of 8x10 photos to sign.
As the couple reached the booth, Reba reached for a photo,
grabbed her pen and, with a smile wider than the Okla-
homa-Texas border, prepared to sign the picture. "Howdy,"
she greeted them, enthused that someone finally wanted to
meet her. "I'm Reba McEntire."

"Ma'am," asked the man politely. "Could you tell me where the men's room is?"

Shattered, and suddenly wondering if she had chosen the wrong vocation, Reba pointed toward the restroom signs. As the couple said thanks and wandered off, she finally put down her Sharpie and almost laid to rest some of her dreams.

Similar scenes take place during every International Country Music Fan Fair—the annual country music extravaganza staged in Nashville. Nowadays when Reba occupies a booth, fans stampede toward it. And they want more than Reba's directions to the restroom. They want a photo with her or an autographed picture or CD. They also scurry to other hot stars like Tim McGraw, Martina McBride, John Michael Montgomery and Faith Hill, ignoring Tex and Tina Nobody whose hearts, lives and desires are laying exposed on the table tops along with their piles of un-requested glossy photos. Some of these talents, near-talents or no-talents will call it quits and head back to their day jobs in the coming months and years. Others, like Reba at Fan Fair '76, will courageously continue to put their hearts and souls on the line, night after night, for more brutal rejection or the slim chances of possible breakthrough success in the future.

It's not an easy life en route to an easy life. There is no such animal as an overnight success in this business. Some cite Billy Ray Cyrus's meteoric rise to stardom with "Achy Breaky Heart." But they ignore a dues-paying decade of playing rough and rumble Kentucky nightclubs filled with more smoke than sentiment, more noise than music, more despair than encouragement. From Tammy Wynette to Alan Jackson, the road has been long, winding, less traveled and littered with enough dead ends and road kills to demolish lesser spirits.

From the Cheap Seats to the Stage

Tracy Lawrence remembers when he sat in the cheap seats way in the back rows at a Shreveport coliseum concert, catching his favorite act, George Strait.

"I didn't have the money to get good tickets," he told me. "So here I was, a poor little boy, a skinny kid from Arkansas and Texas, sitting way in the back of the coliseum."

Years later, Lawrence knew he had made it when he played the same building as the opening act for his hero George Strait. "I looked up into those seats where I had spun my dreams when I was a kid," Tracy told me, his voice growing soft with the memory. "And it really hit me hard. I was standing where George Strait had stood—the guy that had so much influence on me. And I knew then that I had arrived. It's so overwhelming when you work so hard and dream so long. It actually brought tears to my eyes."

Chesnutt Makes His Mark

In a dingy Texas honky-tonk that would make the fabled *Star Wars* bar look like an upscale establishment, a teenager sang his songs night after night. No one applauded or paid much attention. The talk and laughter often overpowered the music coming from the stage. The clank of beer bottles and heavy burger plates thrust on the tables by waitresses provided dissonant sounds that turned each night into a downer for the struggling kid on stage.

Mark Chesnutt, trying to take his music career higher than his father Bob's brief Nashville recording stint, kept singing through it all. Though no one else, beyond his family and a few friends, shared his faith, somehow he believed in himself enough to make it through these dire gigs. So he sang through the turbulence, conquered the trauma and faced his nightly minimum wage set with grit, determination and a belief that better days were coming. All those songs, all those nights, and still not one patron thought he deserved applause. This beer joint was becoming a tear joint.

Then on one night that has been indelibly etched on his memory, Mark Chesnutt heard it—the sound of clapping after he finished a heartfelt ballad. It stopped the struggling singer dead in his tracks.

He actually halted his performance to acknowledge it. "Thank you, thank you," he said, trying to peer through the darkness of the noisy, smoky din to find his first fan, the first person to give him a much needed shot of encouragement.

Mark's eyes finally found the source of the sound. It was a man in a cowboy hat. He wasn't applauding, but was slapping the bottom of a bottle, garnishing his cheeseburger with gobs of ketchup.

So much for applause. Mark took a deep breath and began his next number, still waiting for the cheers that he hoped someday would come his way.

Chapter 2

Stars on Parade

Blake Shelton, Beauty Queen

With hits like "Austin" and "Heavy Liftin'," Blake Shelton rates as one of the hottest new rising stars on the country music horizon. But don't be surprised if you sometime see posters at his concerts announcing:

REWARD! $1,000 (OR WHATEVER YOU WANT) FOR RETURN OF MISSING VIDEOTAPE. CONTACT BLAKE SHELTON, C/O WARNER BROS. RECORDS, NASHVILLE

As Paul Harvey would say, "And now, the rest of the story..."

Shelton can't wait to get his hands on a valuable videotape of his first stage performance at the tender age of eight years old. And if he gets it back, Blake knows exactly what he wants to do with it.

The drama behind the lost tape involves childhood trauma that transcends into Blake's adult life. He explains:

Blake Shelton
(© Warner Bros. Records Inc.)

"I used to sing in my bedroom all the time, and my mom heard me in there and thought I was cute. So she entered me into a beauty pageant when I was eight years old. It was the first time I ever stepped on stage. And it was with 50 little girls!

"I was totally embarrassed and humiliated, and I didn't want any of my friends to know about it. I was in the talent portion with all those girls who were the same age as me. But they were *girls*, man, they were *little girls*! That's what killed me. When a boy is eight years old, you don't like girls. I know *I* didn't. I told Mom I didn't want to sing any more after that because it's too embarrassing.

"That's a good way *not* to start off a career. Honestly, I blocked it out of my mind, so I don't know how I did. I sure didn't come in first in the swimsuit division, and I sure didn't win Miss Congeniality.

"Bless her heart, my mom just wanted me to do something. She was doing what she could just to get me in front of people. She was so proud of that videotape of me on stage in that beauty pageant and was heartbroken when it disappeared."

So, if someone finds the long lost videotape and returns it to Blake Shelton, he'll quickly give it back to his mother, huh? That's what I asked Blake.

"No, it wouldn't go back to her," Blake answered. "I was thanking God that she lost it. I don't want there to be any evidence of that appearance on the pageant. If I find it, I'm going to burn it."

Reba and Red—Friends First

Singing the national anthem helped Reba McEntire launch her show business career with a flurry of stars and stripes.

Red Steagall, riding high in the saddle back in 1974 with "Someone Cares For You," discovered another red-headed country singer at the National Rodeo Finals in Oklahoma City. A freckle-faced rodeo competitor named Reba McEntire wowed Steagall with her stirring performance of the "Star-Spangled Banner."

"I cut a demo with Reba and helped her get her first record deal and kind of advised her along the way," Red recalls. "But more than anything, I was her friend. You have to be friends first, and we definitely are friends. I just love her to death and would do anything for her, and she'd do anything for me.

"Our business relationship was very limited. She'd call me for advice occasionally. It wasn't a manager/client relationship at all, and never was intended to be. It was truly friends first.

"Back then she was exactly the same person that she is now. She knew exactly what she wanted to do. She had tremendous confidence, and, of course, she is one of the most talented people the world will ever know—just a sweet, kind, caring human being. She's still that same person she was back when I saw her at the National Finals in 1974. Her world has changed, and the way people look at her has changed because she is now a superstar.

However, Reba later made one major change—her attitude about starting a family. Her son Shelby is now the delight of her existence, but when I visited her Stringtown, Oklahoma, ranch for a *People* story back in 1984, Reba definitely wasn't in the maternal mindset.

"One of the main reasons I'll never have children is that kids nowadays have no respect for their elders," she told me. Rattled by family gatherings populated by scampering nephews and nieces, Reba made a joking confession:

"After they're gone, I go in the bathroom and eat a whole package of birth control pills."

That attitude changed dramatically with the birth of Shelby, enhancing her family life with husband Narvel Blackstock.

Patriotism Prevails

While the Dixie Chicks dropped a bombshell on themselves with Natalie Maines's controversial claim of shame that the Chicks hailed from the same state as President Bush, other country acts have proudly and profitably waved the flag in a winning way.

Counterpointing the Chicks' comments during America's battle against terrorism and the Saddam Hussein regime in Iraq, Darryl Worley jumped in the fray with his pro-war hit "Have You Forgotten?" The single rode the top of *Billboard's* Hot Country Singles & Tracks chart for several weeks while the similarly titled album made its debut at No. 1 on the trade magazine's Top Country Albums list. Worley wrote the song after he visited U.S. soldiers in Afghanistan, and the Iraqi conflict made it even more relevant.

Toby Keith felt a tingling in his toes after the September 11, 2001, attacks—and it wasn't the "Boot Scootin' Boogie" he wanted to do. Instead he wanted to tap dance on the Taliban terrorists in his fiery "Courtesy of the Red, White & Blue (The Angry American)"—another musical missile launched onto the charts.

The best of the lot was Alan Jackson's contemplative, low-key masterpiece of mournful reaction that perfectly caught the mood of post-9/11 America: "Where Were You (When the World Stopped Turning)?"

These ballads are just the tip of the sand dune. The Warren Brothers scored with "Hey, Mr. President," Clint Black

Toby Keith
(© Dreamworks Records, Inc.)

released "I Raq and Roll," and Aaron Tippin, who jumpstarted his career with the feisty Top Ten hit "You've Got to Stand for Something," returned to the ballad battlefield after September 11, letting fly with "Where the Stars and Stripes and the Eagles Fly." Some critics charge that the artists might be more interested in padding their billfolds than praising the troops—an opinion that Tippin fights. "If anybody wants to whup up on me about that," he told *Billboard*, "they'll have to check my financial statements to see how much I donated to the Red Cross." Tippin's single reportedly raised some $250,000 for that agency.

Lee Greenwood rules as the long-term flag-waving veteran—his "God Bless the USA 2003" enjoyed chart success similar to the original release of the song back in 1984.

U.S. Army Special Forces Staff Sergeant Barry Sadler proved to be the Lee Greenwood of the Vietnam War. His tribute "The Ballad of the Green Berets" hit the top of the pop charts and No. 2 on the country charts. His life, unfortunately, followed a violent path. Sadler was injured when a booby trap exploded in Vietnam, he suffered brain damage when shot in the head during a later robbery attempt at his home in Guatemala, and he died of heart failure in 1989 back in Tennessee.

War-themed hits also include Ernest Tubb's first No. 1 record—"Soldier's Last Letter"—during the World War II era in 1944.

Clint Eastwood, Country Crooner

"Go ahead, make my day!" Clint Eastwood challenged in one of his more memorable movie lines. But country music made Clint's day when he hit the charts in 1980. His duet with Ray Charles, "Beers to You," hailed from Clint's film *Any Which Way You Can*. Eastwood's pairings with Merle Haggard took him to the top of the charts: "Misery and Gin" peaked at No. 3, and "Bar Room Buddies" rocketed all the way to No. 1. Both came from the movie *Bronco Billy*.

So what is Hollywood's favorite movie tough guy like in person? I met Clint in New Orleans for a screening of *Bronco Billy*, and I'm delighted to report that he was one of the friendliest stars—movie or music—that I've ever interviewed.

Movie tough guy Clint Eastwood and his then-lady Sondra
Locke share a laugh with Gerry Wood when he informs
Clint that Sondra will have to return to Tennessee with him.
(Photo courtesy of Gerry Wood)

During a party following the movie, Clint introduced me to his lady at the time, actress Sondra Locke, a native of Tennessee. I turned the tough-guy tables on Clint, put my arm around her shoulder and told him, "I'm sorry, Clint, Sondra's from Tennessee, and she's going to have to come back with me."

Both of them cracked up.

Rascal Flatts
(© Lyric Street Records)

Rascal Flatts Looks Sharp

When those handsome young rascals—Gary LeVox, Jay DeMarcus and Joe Don Rooney—joined forces to form Rascal Flatts, many critics thought they were a ripoff of the "boy band" craze filtering down from the rock world. But their ballad "I'm Movin' On" displayed the trio's credentials as solid talents, worthy of the CMA's Horizon Award.

Perhaps even more nerve-wracking for artists and their record labels than the debut album release is the second album. Was the debut a fluke? Will the sophomore album stiff? Not for Rascal Flatts. That album—*Melt*—entered *Billboard's* chart at No. 1, selling more than 160,000 copies, then went on to achieve platinum status of more than a million sold just five weeks after it hit the marketplace. That's the second best sophomore debut album success in a Nielsen SoundScan listing that placed the Rascals behind the No. 1-ranking Dixie Chicks with *Fly*.

The No. 3 to No. 20 positions go to—in this order—LeAnn Rimes, Tim McGraw, John Michael Montgomery, keith urban, Billy Ray Cyrus, Jessica Andrews, Wynonna, Nickel Creek, Brooks & Dunn, Darryl Worley, Blackhawk, Brad Paisley, Rebecca Lynn Howard, Deana Carter, Tracy Lawrence, Faith Hill and Clay Walker.

keith urban
(© Capitol Records)

How Johnny Cash and
Waylon Jennings Defeated Drugs

The rugged road life of country music makers leads some entertainers down perilous pathways of alcohol and drug abuse. The death of Hank Williams at age 29 on the first day of 1953 should have served as a wake-up call, but the phone lines were busy for several stars caught in the same addictive trap as Hank.

One of the saddest losses was Keith Whitley, who also lived his lyrics and died. He was riding a string of three No. 1 hits when he reached the fateful day of May 9, 1989. On the morning of that day, Keith's mother, stirred by dark premonitions about her son, called him at 9:30 a.m. from Sandy Hook, Kentucky. "He sounded so tired," she told me. "We had a good talk, but I still had those feelings."

Keith's sister experienced an even stranger forewarning on that same morning when she glanced at the color photo of Keith in her living room. Keith was flashing that shy smile in the picture, but suddenly, the colors vanished from the photo—the color disappearing completely from his face until it became a whiter shade of pale. Shocked, his sister shook her head, looked away, blinked and then looked back. Once again, the picture of Keith was in color.

From the time of the mother's phone conversation with Keith and his sister's viewing of the changing photograph to a few hours later at high noon, something dreadful happened. Keith Whitley died.

Alcohol poisoning snuffed out the bright light at age 33, and the falling star left behind his widow, Lorrie Morgan, a child and a stepchild.

Johnny Cash and Waylon Jennings were more fortunate in combating their drug-induced demons. Addicted to pain-killing pills, Cash no sooner left the Betty Ford Center in Rancho Mirage, California, than he learned about his friend Waylon, who was losing his own war against cocaine. Waylon's wife, Jessi Colter, kept him alive by force-feeding him milkshakes containing fruit, honey, vitamins and proteins.

"Jessi went through hell watching me die," Waylon later told me.

Cash knew his friend wouldn't respond to heavy-handed arguments, noting, "Waylon is his own man, and you can't preach to him."

So Johnny took the subtle approaching, pointing to his own face proudly, saying, "I want to show you my big bright eyes. I want you to know if you decide you need help, I know a good place."

Waylon found his place near Scottsdale, Arizona, walked the mountains and dropped drugs cold turkey.

"Being off drugs kept me high with my family," explained Waylon.

"People gave me credit for Waylon's recovery," said Johnny Cash. "Nobody but Waylon did that."

If At First You Don't Succeed

Rejected by just about every record company in Nashville, the dishwasher/cook/wannabe-singer believed in himself enough to continue his efforts to make the big time. He'd pop out of the grease and smoke of the Nashville Palace nightclub kitchen long enough to perform a couple songs for the audience, then head back to his chores of deep-frying catfish.

Warner Bros. Records had turned him down three times before one of that label's executives, Martha Sharp, fell in love with the singer's voice and potential. Soon, Randy Travis had a major label contract to sign, celebrated his first No. 1 hit with "On the Other Hand" in 1986, and evolved into one of the most important artists in country music history by taking a post-*Urban Cowboy* watered-down version of country music and returning it back to the traditional roots from which it had grown.

Randy was a rounder in his earlier years, landing in jail, high on booze and drugs, and crash-landing a car during a 135-mph police chase.

"It's hard to outrun police," Randy told me. "I ain't never had much luck doing it. They took me down to the jail and locked me up."

Before frying catfish, washing dishes and working construction jobs, Randy toiled at turkey farming, a profession that spooks him to this day.

"Turkeys are absolutely the dumbest animals I've seen in my life," claims Travis. "They'll go out when it's raining and drown."

Cagle Country

With his self-titled album hitting No. 1 and soaring singles like "What a Beautiful Day" crashing the Top Ten, Chris Cagle has emerged as one of the top newcomers in recent years.

Cagle's keen understanding of the country music fan helped fuel his drive to stardom.

Advises Chris: "My audience is blue collar—a factory worker, a nurse, a farmer, oil rig worker, an office worker making too little money for too much work, a housewife, every woman who starves for attention from her man and every man who doesn't know how to give her that attention."

Chris Cagle
(© Capitol Records)

After effectively dissecting his audience, Chris defines his musical mission as "filling that gap between these people and building a bridge with my music."

The gap-filling bridge builder continues his chart-climbing.

Allison Moorer
(© Universal South)

The Most Beautiful Girl in the World

Charlie Rich's biggest hit, "The Most Beautiful Girl" topped both the country and pop charts in 1973.

Which brings to mind the most beautiful women of country music. Who is No. 1?

Take your pick: Faith Hill, Martina McBride, Allison Moorer, Dolly Parton, Patty Loveless, LeAnn Rimes, Jessica Andrews, Stella Parton, Deana Carter, Chalee Tennison, Terri Clark, Kristyn Osborn of SHeDAISY…the list goes on.

My pick? Shania Twain.

Not only does Shania radiate beauty, the Canadian chanteuse combines it with exceptional talent and charm.

Shania's co-writer, producer, and husband, John "Mutt" Lange, carries credentials as one of the top pop producers in the music world. Besides Shania, Lange has produced such acts as Foreigner, Def Leppard and The Cars.

Shania and Dolly Parton have more in common than devastating looks and talent—they also can claim the most camera-shy husbands in show business. Lange and Dolly's husband, Carl Dean, never appear in public with their spouses, whether it's award shows or concerts. Both prefer to stay out of the limelight and away from the camera lens of photographers who could earn big bucks for photos of the couples together.

Shania Twain, Gerry Wood's pick as the most beautiful woman of country music, takes time out for a photo with the author. (Photo courtesy of Gerry Wood)

The Bad Boys of Beaumont

Strange, but the town of Beaumont, Texas, produced two of my all-time favorite personalities in country music, Mark Chestnutt and Tracy Byrd, along with my least favorite, Clay Walker.

Let me explain.

I loved Mark Chesnutt's singing style long before I met him—and I admired him as a person even more when I traveled with him on writing assignments. "Too Cold At Home" and "Almost Goodbye" elevated Mark to classic crooner status, but his stubborn honesty sometimes landed him in hot water with other journalists and fans.

"I put my foot in my mouth both onstage and off quite a few times," Mark confessed to me. "I'm totally honest with people. I don't bullshit anybody—and that's gotten me in trouble."

Couple blunt honesty with the tiring, energy-draining demands of touring, and you've got Mark Chesnutt complaining from coast to coast. "If my daddy had been here, he would have kicked me in the butt," he explained. "It got to where I was tired and had a bad attitude all the time— didn't want to talk to nobody, didn't want to go nowhere. Just wanted to go home where I had my kids and wife that I was never around, and I wanted to be with them so much."

So Mark made some changes, scaling back his touring schedule and other time-gulping career demands. He tried to live what he described as a "normal" life, but that didn't work either.

"I'm not cut out for that," Mark concluded. "I wasn't put here to be a normal person. I try to be a normal dad and a normal husband as much as I can, but at the same time, I've got to be this crazy singer-entertainer to make it all work."

Mark has tweaked his attitude, and paced himself better, and the results rejuvenated his career.

While his outspoken candor turned off others, Mark's truthful nature always impressed me. Mark was so thankful when I arranged for one of his idols, legendary producer and Sun Records owner Sam Phillips, to show up in the studio unexpectedly when we were in Memphis. His eyes were as big as compact discs when Sam walked in the room. Later, over drinks in the lobby of the Peabody Hotel, Mark spent fifteen minutes telling me what an honor it was to meet Phillips.

During a visit to Mark's Texas home, the singer was his candid self. Talking on the phone with a friend, he complained, "The bed of my pickup truck is so dirty, you could grow corn in it."

And while walking his property back to a deer stand, we kept running into swarms of flying insects. I asked him what they were.

"Love bugs," he told me. "See how they're attached? They mate when they fly together like that."

"Wow!" I told him. "I'd crash-land if I tried that."

It took a while to get Mark to quit laughing.

When Mark's pal Tracy Byrd celebrated a platinum album by taking his crew and band on a three-day fishing trip off the Louisiana coast, he invited me along. Three days and nights with these hellraisers offshore in a "house barge" proved to be one fun trip.

Great food, great fishing, great beer, and great Tracy tricks turned our voyage into *American Sportsman Meets Animal House.*

On the last night of the trip, Tracy found some bright red nail polish in a bathroom cabinet and proceeded to paint the toenails of his band members as they slept off the long day of sun and fun.

*Platinum artist Tracy Byrd uses crimson red as he paints the toenails
of Gerry Wood aboard a house barge off the Louisiana coast.
(Photo courtesy of Gerry Wood)*

And not just his band members. When I awoke in the
morning and looked down at my feet, I thought my toes
were bleeding. Every toenail was blood red, thanks to Tracy
Byrd, toenail painter extraordinaire.

The only Beaumont boy I don't care for is Clay Walker.
That stems from an interview I tried to conduct with him
for a story on his new album. It was the most difficult interview session I've ever experienced. Every time I asked Clay a
question, he would answer it in one sentence or, sometimes,
in one word.

"Tell me about your new album," I'd ask.

"It's good."

"What are your favorite cuts on the album?"

"All."

Try to write an article with answers like these.

After frustrating me with non-answers, Clay would look over at his manager and grin, like, "Look what I'm doing—aren't I cute?"

After fifteen minutes of getting absolutely nowhere, I was ready to walk out of the interview. I knew that Mark Chesnutt and Tracy Byrd were close friends, but neither seemed to cozy up to Clay Walker. And I knew that Walker felt very competitive against his fellow Beaumont singers.

"So tell me, Clay, what are your upcoming touring plans?"

"Starts tomorrow." He looked over at his manager again, and grinned.

I turned off my tape recorder. I closed my notebook. I got up and started to leave. But not before saying: "Let me tell you something, Clay. I don't know what your problem is, but I don't have time for this crap, and I'm outta here."

"Wait! What's the matter?"

"You are the worst interview subject I've ever encountered.

"Me?"

"Yes, you. I've been talking to you for fifteen minutes and I don't have one word I can use. You are a worse subject than even Mark Chesnutt!"

His mouth dropped open as I headed to the door.

"Wait! Come back. Let's try again."

I returned, turned on the tape recorder, and opened my writing pad. "Okay, let's start where we began. Tell me about your new album."

Surprisingly, Walker opened up and talked about his new album for ten minutes. Then he delved into his personal life, career and health worries—and I ended up with a strong interview that made for a cover story. His cutesy mode had turned to a courteous mode.

But he still ranks as one of the oddest, most difficult personalities I've had the misfortune to encounter since Janis Joplin. But that's another story for another book.

Tracing His Injuries

It's a wonder that Trace Adkins is still alive.

"It's not the first time I've almost gotten killed," Trace said after his second wife accidentally shot him.

Previous encounters of the worst kind came when Trace suffered severe cuts in a bulldozer accident, leg injuries in

Trace Adkins
(© Capitol Records)

an oil tank explosion, and a finger almost cut off as he tried to open a can with a six-inch knife.

When doctors told Trace he wouldn't be able to bend that finger again, he directed them to fuse the joints in a curve so they'd fit around the neck of his guitar.

Now there's a country music trooper for you!

Michael Martin Murphey Dismounted

Cowboy to the core, Michael Martin Murphey rides horses with confidence—but there's one young mustang that gave him a toss he'll never forget.

"I was on a trail ride down in the beautiful Canadian River Canyon around Cimarron, New Mexico," Michael recalled. "Mustangs generally like to stay with the herd, and this one attached himself to a mule that he really liked. We were riding along and the horse didn't notice that the mule my son was riding was getting farther and farther away. When he turned his head and realized that the mule was far away from him, he took off and started running.

"The bad news was that he was running through trees and eight-foot-tall cactus. He was running so fast I realized he was about to take me through some low branches of cedar trees. I decided I was either going to be beat up by these branches as I was dragged through the trees or else I'd have to jump off my horse while he was running full speed, because he wouldn't stop.

"I got both feet out of the stirrups, pushed myself off the horse and vaulted over the saddle horn—and when I hit the ground, I kept rolling. It surprised my horse so bad that he skidded, stopped, turned around, ran back to me and reared up. When he did, I saw this horse over the top of me with hooves above me. I thought he was trying to kill me. His hooves came down over my body and landed on either side of my chest. He could have killed me if he landed on my chest. He then took off and went for the mule that he wanted to be next to."

After relating that scary tale to me in his cabin near Red River, New Mexico, Michael suggested we go horseback riding along the top of the mountain. He saddled up two horses for us, turned to me and said, "Gerry, I'm going to let you ride my favorite horse, Thunderbolt."

Although I'm from the Bluegrass State of Kentucky, known for its horse farms, I'm still a little uncertain in the saddle. After that description of Michael's runaway horse, and looking at the fidgety, huffing and puffing Thunderbolt, I had second thoughts about this trail ride.

"*Thunderbolt?*" I asked Michael.

"Yes, my favorite, he's the fastest horse I've got."

"Michael," I pleaded. "Don't you have another horse around here for me? Preferably one with the name of *Old Paint?*"

Leading a Dog's Life With Tom T. Hall

One of the most versatile talents in the country music cosmos, Tom T. Hall writes songs for others—Jeannie C. Riley's "Harper Valley PTA"—and for himself. His No. 1 hits include "The Year That Clayton Delaney Died," "(Old Dogs, Children and) Watermelon Wine," and "I Love." He also writes books—everything from songwriting instruction manuals to novels. And he always surrounds himself with a dog or 50.

Tom T.'s wife, Miss Dixie, won ribbons and trophies for the basset hounds she raised and trained on their 80-acre

Fox Hollow Plantation outside Nashville. When Dixie established the Animal and Humane Shelter in nearby Franklin, Tom T. held fundraising events for the cause.

Tom T. told me why he loves dogs.

"They don't have any religion, they don't have any politics," he explained. "So we don't have anything to argue about."

Plaques in the two-story home bear such canine-friendly maxims as "This house is maintained entirely for the comfort and convenience of our dogs," and "The more people I meet, the more I love my dog."

One of Tom T.'s friends, Hank Cochran, learned that it's risky to drink too much at a Fox Hollow party. Writer of such classics as Eddy Arnold's "Make the World Go Away" and the Patsy Cline evergreen "I Fall to Pieces," a tipsy Hank stretched out on an oriental rug in the Hall's recreation room and soon fell asleep. When the party was over, Tom T. didn't want Hank driving home in that condition, so he rolled up the songwriter in the huge carpet and tossed it, with Hank snoring away inside, atop the pool table.

"Make the World Go Away" was probably the theme song running through Cochran's bleary, bloodshot eyes when he awoke the next morning, wrapped in an oriental rug atop the green felt of a pool table.

Brad Paisley and the Loser's Lullaby

"It's something that every guy has been through," explained Brad Paisley, co-writer of the ultimate romantic rejection song, "Me Neither." "If you haven't been through this, you haven't lived!"

Brad wrote the humorous ditty with Chris DuBois and Frank Rogers during a nine-hour drive from South Carolina to Nashville. All three were single guys, and all had suffered negative moments in the dating game.

Rogers sat in the back seat, plunking on his guitar. DuBois drove and Brad rode shotgun. They started swapping tales about love gone wrong, and the song was finished on Interstate 40 "somewhere between Knoxville and Nashville."

The ballad takes a whimsical look at the drama of trying to start a relationship with the opposite sex, and it caught fire as one of the fan favorite choices off his debut album *Who Needs Pictures.*

"It wasn't my biggest hit," Brad noted. "But it's the one that folks love to see me do live."

George Strait: They Don't Come Better

As a performer and as a person, George Strait is as talented and friendly as they come. He is also one of the most private entertainers in show business when it comes to his home life.

George, a shoo-in for future Country Music Hall of Fame induction, once was quoted as saying he would rather go to the dentist and undergo a root canal than to give an interview. Thanks to a 26-page *Billboard* magazine tribute to George that I produced, I acquired the distinction of conducting more face-to-face interviews with the reclusive star than any other writer. That's a questionable honor, because I've done just a handful of sit-down sessions with George.

But it wasn't until an interview with George in the Nashville office of his manager Erv Woolsey that he gave me the reason for his penchant for privacy. And it was the first time he had ever brought up the heartbreaking tragic death of his 13-year-old daughter, Jenifer.

I started off by telling George that I had planned to bring my dentist friend, Dr. Pegg, with me so he could have the choice between experiencing a root canal or talking to me for an interview. When I showed him a photo of Dr. Pegg, a gorgeous lady dentist from Cleveland, Ohio, he thought even more strongly about the root canal.

George laughed, then his movie star handsome face warmed with that killer smile of his. But then he grew serious, and I knew he had something he wanted to talk about.

"I got real private after I lost my daughter," he confided. "I really shut things down right then."

In all my past interviews with George, I did not bring up this topic of losing his daughter in a 1986 car accident. He appreciated me not probing into a topic that others always questioned him about. I think that's why I was the first one he discussed Jenifer's death with.

"I felt that nothing worse could happen to me," George said, his eyes growing sad with the memory of parents coping with the death of their child. "I didn't feel like talking to anyone who wasn't close to me. I decided that was the way I was going to handle my career. If it worked, great, and if it didn't work, then I knew that nothing worse could happen than what had already taken place."

George abided by his decision, and for more than a year he refused all interview requests. Even before the accident, Strait shielded his family and private life from the constant spotlight of attention that stardom often ignites.

"I need another life besides the one when I'm a country entertainer," he said. "Privacy is so important to me, and it's important for my wife Norma and son, George, Jr., to have that, too. It's important for them to have as normal a life as possible."

George on stage and George at home on his Texas ranch are two different Georges.

"I don't want to always be the country music singer," he stressed. "Especially when I'm at home."

Our groundbreaking interview that started with a laugh ended the same way when I asked him about his ranch.

"How many acres is it?" I asked.

"Oh, I can't really tell you that," George answered.

"Come on, George. I heard it's over 8,000 acres. Is that true?"

George smiled away the answer.

"Okay, is it all right if I say it's over forty acres?" I persisted.

"Yeah, Gerry," Strait said, agreeing to the forty-acre concept. "You can say it's over forty acres."

That winning smile crossed George Strait's face again as we finished the toughest interview he had ever given.

George Strait—onstage or at home—is as good as it gets.

Chapter 3

Up Close and Personal: Fan Fair Frenzy

Garth Brooks, Marathon Man

"Ladies and gentlemen, Mick Jagger and the Rolling Stones are now in booth number 18 signing autographs and posing for photos."

"At booth 23, the Red Hot Chili Peppers are now welcoming all their fans for pictures, signings and chats."

"Attention. At booth 40, Madonna is signing her CDs and posters—she'll stay later in case the line moves slowly."

"For those who want a meet-and-greet with Eminem, he plans to remain in his fan club booth all night just to get to know his audience better, kiss babies and sign copies of his new album, *Mama Taught Me Best*."

A rock 'n' roll fan's heaven? Oh, yes! Of course, it'll never happen. But this is exactly what transpires annually in a defining event in the rituals of country music—the International Country Music Fan Fair held beneath the blazing summer sun in Nashville.

Eninem and his buddies won't be there—or attending any function anywhere resembling this fans-meet-stars extravaganza—but the country acts will sign, pose, chat, and often stay until the last request from the last fan is granted. Garth Brooks once spent an entire night into the next daybreak doing just that, not even taking a bathroom break.

Nothing more powerfully typifies the extra mile that country stars travel for their faithful fans than this spectacle where artists are not only approachable, but touchable, huggable, photographable, lovable and downright downhomeable. Rising stars and starlets join the giants of show business participating in the shows and sideshows of Fan Fair. The event allows fans from around the globe—Japan, Germany, England, Russia and 25 other countries—to go face to face, eyeball to eyeball with their favorites. Close encounters of the best kind. Female fans can plant a kiss on the cheeks of Marty Stuart, Alan Jackson, Ty Herndon and Tracy Byrd while the men can snuggle up to Lorrie Morgan, Martina McBride and Faith Hill for a photo that will assume a prominent display position once they get back home.

Here's the Beef!

The statistics are staggering: Some 90 acts perform on stage during the four-day festival, almost 200 exhibition booths hawk stars and their merchandise, and snap-happy shutterbugs shoot an estimated 70,000 photographs. But their hunger isn't limited to music alone. They wolf down 13,000 pounds of barbecue smoked to perfection by the

Tim McGraw
(© Curb Records)

roving ambassadors from Texas—the Odessa Chuck Wagon Gang.

From college professors to dropouts, grandparents to babies, rich to poor, white to black (with all shades in between), they flock to their Mecca in Nashville. Kris Kristofferson summed up the surging crowd's diversity by comparing it to the audience at a Willie Nelson concert: "Rockers to farmers to bikers and lawyers, white collar, blue collar, no collar."

All of the faithful are sweltering in Tennessee's simmering solstice season, and loving it, each drop of sweat that trickles down their forehead forms a liquid tribute to the music and the music makers they love. Heat indexes that have soared to the 100-degree range, spiced by thunderstorms booming suddenly out of nowhere, would soak and sink the spirits of lesser mortals. But country music fans, like their idols, are not lesser mortals.

Sporting T-shirts, caps, and sometimes tattoos that hawk their favorites, the Fan Fair tribe descends on their field of dreams, formerly the Tennessee State Fairgrounds, and now centered around the downtown Nashville home turf of the Tennessee Titans NFL football team—the Coliseum. They parade in the line that snakes around the front of the stage for a photo of Neal McCoy or Tim McGraw or Shania Twain—from three feet away.

The personal touch of the fan/star interaction illustrates what's best about country music, why it appeals to the masses and why a fan who has touched, or been touched, by Vince Gill will be moved by that magic moment forever and will purchase his CDs and attend his concerts. The ritual—for both fans and artists—draws more than 20,000 of country music's faithful.

Vince Gill, Invincible on the Charity Circuit

Why do country performers go so far above and beyond the call of duty when it comes to those who support their careers? It's not just Fan Fair, it's 24/7/365 as they take to the road in an armada of luxury buses, some playing more than 200 dates a year throughout the U.S. and Canada, and an increasing international penetration.

They sing through sickness, exhaustion, and personal problems, then they'll often mingle with fans backstage and find time for charity causes in their precious few down hours. Perhaps it's because they grew up idolizing stars who knew what their fans wanted, both on and off the stage—and gave it to them. Maybe it's because country music is agrarian-based—and country folks always had time for a howdy and a chat with neighbors and friends. Possibly it's just because they're damn decent people with hearts bigger than their egos.

And…perhaps it's all of the above.

More than anyone else, Vince Gill exemplifies the giving spirit of the country music community. He has played in the City of Hope celebrity softball game, tosses hoops in an annual charity basketball game and sponsors two Nashville area golf tournaments—The Vinny and the Mini-Vinny to raise funds for Tennessee Junior Golf. The Vinny draws top professionals such as John Daly, who has won the British Open, along with top country stars for two days of golfing greatness and goofiness. The Mini-Vinny attracts junior golfers—hailing from suburbs to inner-city housing projects—who are paired on the links with country music stars.

"I never dreamed that The Vinny would grow to this magnitude," Vince told me as I walked the course with him during one of his tourneys. He looked beyond the green at the 18th hole where a huge gallery—composed of golf fans, music fans and a hybrid mixture of both—applauded and shrieked at the appropriate moments. "Everywhere I go, fans and the public are asking about it."

One of the invitational's celebrities, Kix Brooks of Brooks and Dunn, offered the ultimate tribute to the tourney's founder and father. "I've never seen anyone like Vince Gill," praised Brooks. "When we get back from a really long and exhausting concert tour and I go home to recoup, I turn on the TV and there's Vince—just back from a long tour of his own—at still another charity event. That man is amazing."

Sometimes the strain and stress takes its toll. Pills and booze and drugs have nudged some entertainers over the edge. Some made it back by clinging to the precipice and hauling themselves up, often with the help of friends, family and support groups. Some didn't make it back. But for every tragic ending of a Hank Williams or Keith Whitley, there's a Johnny Cash or George Jones proving that, yes, you can survive.

And there's always a Vince Gill to prove that you can handle the pressure with no more serious after-effects than an occasional toss of a golf club after an errant shot falls in the rough. "I've golfed 23 straight times without throwing a single club," Vince once told me, the only time he has been known to brag about himself. "I'm really keeping my temper under control out there."

The constant charitable enterprises of the entertainers and the remarkable pilgrimage called Fan Fair reinforce the special nature of this unique musical genre.

It's an odd mixture of personalities, lifestyles and philosophies. But, year after year, it works. And that's what counts.

Chapter 4

Love and Loveless
Ride the Santa Train

Round the mountain and down the tracks
Santa's Train is coming back
Filled with presents for me and you
Christmas is coming, that's for sure!

Hear that whistle, hear that moan
Here comes Santa, he's not alone
Stars and helpers heave the goods
Grab one quick and back to the woods!

—Theme song from the novel in progress, *The Santa Train Surprise,* by Gerry Wood ©2003, Beagle Brothers Music, BMI

The careers and lives of country stars create a lifetime of memories—humorous, sad, tragic, triumphant, and various shades in between.

Covering these special people for books, magazines, television and radio has led me to some of the most soul-stirring moments of my life. The most emotion-packed expedition transported me back to my Kentucky homeland when Patty Loveless returned to her birthplace and rode the rails on the *Santa Special*. The annual passenger train voyage, dating back to 1943, pulls out of the Pikeville, Kentucky, region and snakes southbound through the mountains of the Bluegrass State and Virginia, before reaching Kingsport, Tennessee, the terminal for its 110-mile trek.

What makes the *Special* so special is its mission. Called "the world's longest Santa parade," the 11-car train is a joint goodwill venture of CSX Transportation and the Kingsport Chamber of Commerce. As the Christmas choo-choo makes 15 stops along its slow and winding way from the morning departure to afternoon arrival seven hours later, Santa Claus and his helpers occupy the rear platform, tossing out more than 20 tons of presents. Children, parents, grandparents, and even homeless wayfarers swarm the train en route, arriving with sacks for their holiday haul and leaving with everything from candy and books to plush teddy bears and dolls, hurled into their hands by Santa and his ever-present elves.

Santa's Sweetest Elf

Santa Claus always needs some assistance for this demanding job, and Patty Loveless volunteered to help Saint Nick with these duties in 1999 and 2002. Before her first trip aboard the *Santa Special*, she had no idea about the emotions and memories it would trigger. A native of Pikeville, Patty recalled her youth when she observed the

Patty Loveless tosses a teddy bear from the Santa Claus Special train.
(Photo courtesy of Gerry Wood)

excited countenances of the children catching the gifts she tosses their way.

"It makes me happy, and it makes me want to cry at the same time," she told me between sessions of flinging presents to the proud, but sometimes poor, children of the Appalachians. "I lived here; these are my roots. When I see myself as a child in the faces of these kids, it makes me want to cry—I've been fighting back tears all day. One little girl told me she didn't want anything for herself, just a doll for her sister."

The crowd cheered the redheaded beauty, a homegrown success story from their very own hills and valleys. The thrilling Christmas season communion turned from a one-way joyful mission into a two-way street of love as Patty glanced along the tracks. She spotted a small child held high by grandparents, and the tot blew her a kiss. On the front porch of a gray farmhouse stood an old veteran wearing his military uniform proudly as he brandished an American flag with his left hand, and with his right hand formed a curt salute to Santa and the train. The sight and sound that really got to Patty, though, was the skinny kid in blue jeans and T-shirt who tipped his blue and white University of Kentucky cap at her and yelled, "Thanks, neighbor!"

"That says it all," Patty said, turning to me, her voice breaking with emotion. "*Neighbor*. There's something about the Christmas season and people coming together to do something like this that our world needs much more of." The train lurched forward for more stops ahead in small towns with the fetching names of Dante, Dungannon, Speer's Ferry and Toms Bottom. "It's not so much the presents that are being thrown off the train as it is the wonderful spirit of giving."

Why the World Loves Loveless

I informed Patty, a gold and platinum artist, about the extra excitement she brought to the *Santa Special* with her presence on the platform as Santa's helper. Locals looked with pleasure and pride at the woman from their own neck of the woods who made it to the top of the country music world. Patty's participation spoke volumes to these hardy mountain folks.

"I've always looked at myself as a singer, and not a famous person or star," she continued, with not a hint of mock modesty. "Many artists have stirred my emotions with their

Patty Loveless
(© Sony Music Entertainment Inc.)

songs and music, and that's helped me through many things in my life. And that's what I want to do—move people and make them feel those same emotions. Artists need to stay true to who they are and what they're about. I love singing pure country and bluegrass and I like to rock a little, too."

The magic of passenger trains hooked a new passenger. Patty huddled with her producer-husband Emory Gordy, Jr. to plan a later Amtrak trip along the west coast. As the *Santa Special* rumbled into another town, Patty paid tribute to her Appalachian homeland. "There's a lot of soul in these mountains," she said, her eyes growing moist again as she gazed at the soothing scene of a crystal blue stream winding along the tracks and the dark green pine trees rimming the highest ridge of the hills. "That's why a lot of soulful music comes from here."

The train whistle heralded the arrival of the *Santa Special* in Waycross, Tennessee. Patty scrambled through the passenger cars and gift-filled baggage car to once again join Santa on the back observation platform, smile on her face, love in her heart and a fuzzy teddy bear in her hands, where it would not stay for long.

Loveless saw a thin girl, perhaps about ten years old, shyly standing far in the distance, away from the nearby mob that surged to the train. Patty's childhood surged to life again in the form of that youngster. With the grace and power of a major-league baseball pitcher, she cocked her arm back and hurled the teddy bear on a skyward loop to her intended receiver. The mountain angel snagged the furry missile and clutched it to her chest like a long-lost friend. The child's cherubic face glowed with the brilliance and sheen of a Christmas candle, creating a portrait of joy that will provide mental music for Patty for as long as she lives, for as long as there is a Santa Claus, for as long as there is a *Santa Special,* and for as long as there is a Christmas.

The whistle blew long and loud, and, steel wheels to steel rails, Santa's railroad sleigh smoothly glided off to the next stop.

On the back platform, waving goodbye to the disappearing crowd, stood two tired but triumphant figures, their arms aching from the day's toy tossing. But no one was complaining.

Santa Claus gave his favorite country singer a gentle kiss on the cheek when he saw a tear slide down her smiling face. "You did great, Patty," he said. "We'll have to get you back here next year."

"You won't have to ask me twice," responded Patty, brushing away the tear, her long day beginning to fade into the treasure chest of her memory.

Patty's countenance grew purely angelic at the thought of returning to these rails. She gave Santa a big hug just so he'd remember his promise.

Ol' Saint Nick can expect one lovely Kentucky songbird by his side when the whistle blows its sound of hope and happiness, signaling the beginning of another journey that fulfills dreams both on and off this very special train.

Chapter 5

A Defining Moment...
What IS Country?

Pop Goes the Country

Thanks to the Vesuvius-like eruption of country music, it's difficult to tell who the players are without a scorecard. Sometimes it's even hard to discern whether it's country music or...pop...rock...soul...blues...folk...

Shania Twain shows up in clothes so scanty they would make a bikini blush. Her concerts have about as much country feel as a Las Vegas glitter and glamour show, but somehow the gorgeous and talented thrush manages to please both country and pop audiences, selling millions of albums and selling out concerts.

More polished and devastating with the passage of each day, Faith Hill tiptoes across the same high wire, balancing both aspects of her career perfectly...so far. Arms outstretched as she treads perilously high above the Gulf of

Faith Hill
(© Warner Bros. Records Inc.)

Collapsed Careers, her left hand clutches a gold record and her right hand holds a platinum album award. Faith moves ahead confidently, knowing her career has never been hotter.

Reba McEntire personifies a country music star who knows how to diversify her entertainment achievements into many facets of show business. When I first met her, she was a freckle-faced, barrel-racing rodeo champ who sang on the side. After her coronation as a queen of country music, Reba looked for more challenges, pursued them, and met them. Unashamedly picking pop material for her distinctive twang-inflected interpretations, Reba expanded into elaborate stage productions involving multiple set and costume changes. She wowed New York City's Broadway audiences with her critically acclaimed role in *Annie Get Your Gun*. She moved to television with a popular network show named after the single name she now uses: *Reba*.

Billy Ray Cyrus and Sawyer Brown's Mark Miller gyrate with fluid on-stage movements—their high-stepping, prancing spurred rumors of stints as Chippendale dancers. Shelby Lynne veered onto the side streets of big band music with a 14-piece orchestra behind her, just one of the reinventions of her singing style. Shelby is not the only big band fancier who has scored on the country charts. No singer is more traditionally based than George Strait. But George once confided to me that he would love to cut a big band album some day.

Other country acts transcend genres by singing while backed by huge symphonic orchestras. Emmylou Harris, Willie Nelson and Michael Martin Murphey have created a whole new sound for their music this way.

Willie, of course, is the poster boy for trying everything. His duet partners have ranged from Julio Iglesias to Lee

Lee Ann Womack
(© MCA Nashville)

Ann Womack. His music embraces country, rock, folk, jazz, blues, and other styles. And it all sounds good.

Alison Krauss remains unabashedly bluegrass with her sensitive, vulnerable wisp of a voice while Dwight Yoakam takes country back to his core Kentucky roots while adding a fresh, almost mystical, twist with his albums and super cool look.

Garth Falls into a Burning Ring of Fire

Garth Brooks proved he was willing to swing from the nearest chandelier or scaffold rung, fight fire with actual fire from the stage, romp, roam, ruin good guitars with a shattering ferocity that would make The Who proud and sail high over his concert audiences while singing. He revolutionized country music production and sales totals while contributing meaningful, lasting classics such as "If Tomorrow Never Comes" and "The Dance." Although deemed by most as a failure, his Chris Gaines experiment to slip into the alter ego of a rock star left some good music behind. It was a bold and courageous move. Who knows where the next career turn will take him? He loves playing the Grand Ole Opry, but some of his stage antics would have puzzled Roy Acuff, who, it must be admitted, frequently balanced a fiddle bow on his nose and demonstrated his prowess with the yo-yo during instrumental breaks in his songs. How to honor a U.S. president when he visits the Grand Ole Opry? Do as Roy did. Yank out your yo-yo and give the chief executive a lesson in how to use it—as he did during President Richard M. Nixon's visit during the heat of the Watergate scandal.

With a powerful voice worthy of grand opera as well as the Grand Ole Opry, John Berry says that his brother sings opera in New York. No surprise, since those sonorous vocal cords run deep in the Berry family.

No wonder country music is so hard to define. As an original American art form—with a bow to its British Empire origins transplanted to the Appalachian mountain folk—the genre reflects this country's amalgamation of lifestyles, races, creeds and cultures.

We can discover what Roy Orbison might have sounded

like had he grown up in Cuba as we listen to Raul Malo's glorious vocals for The Mavericks, hailing from the Cuban-American and rock clubs of Miami. The off-again, on-again nature of the group gives Malo a chance to show his impressive pipes as a solo act. The Canadian chanteuse, k.d. lang—she of the lower-case non-capitalization style preferred also by keith urban—weaves in and out of country music. She's joined by her north-of-the-border cohorts who hit more charts than just country—Anne Murray, Michelle Wright and the aforementioned, but worth mentioning again, Shania Twain.

Mary Chapin Carpenter with her compelling musical stories could, like Kathy Mattea, pass for a folk singer, while Terri Clark, like David Ball, mines the promising shafts of pure in-your-face country, following the tradition of Loretta Lynn. Wynonna Judd loves leaning toward rock but will never be mistaken for Grace Slick, thanks to her in-the-genes musical education from mother Naomi. Like Wynonna, Hank Williams Jr. and Travis Tritt can rock with the best of them but can also render country ballads with gritty perfection.

Chicks: Roasted...Fried...Done?

And then there are the...Dixie Chicks! We know where they've been. Talented Texas beauties with sassy Natalie Maines curling her distinctive style around the lyrics as her mates play up a storm. It's where the Chicks are *going* that has many country fans scratching their heads.

Soon after switching their allegiance from the Nashville music executives who directed their career to top of the charts, they took a sharp left turn for the left coast in efforts to expand the dimensions of their future career. Sometimes this works for country acts convinced that Hollywood agents, bookers and management offer better opportunities for television and movie dreams. Sometimes it doesn't work. For the Dixie Chicks, circa 2003, the jury is still out.

Perhaps we should say "circus 2003," regarding the Chicks. Natalie Maines's Bush-blasting comments drew cheers in England on the eve of the U.S./Iraq war. But it didn't play well in most areas back in her home state, home country, and home music category. Talk radio lines lit up coast to coast with caustic Chick-crunching comments. Jay Leno enjoyed a field day with Dixie Chick jokes about lost fans and declining record sales. The trio definitely lost thousands of fans. But they also might have gained thousands more with all the attention and publicity generated by the media feeding frenzy.

No sooner than one controversy seemed to be dying down a bit, along came the Dixie Chicks naked on the *Entertainment Weekly* cover. Though chicken breasts were discretely hidden by other parts of the nude bodies, the cover sent shock waves into the country music world once again. But if the idea was to draw attention to a group that can back up their high-profile attitude with high-powered performancees, then they succeeded. Again, the jury is still out.

What Goes Around Comes Around

Similar to other styles of music, the fads and fashions of the listening, viewing, and album-purchasing public impact country music, sometimes positively, other times with negative results. The *Urban Cowboy* craze back at the turn of the

1980s proved that country music gone astray can ultimately result in a sad sight, not to mention a sorrowful sound.

To its credit, country music provides common ground for all the influences that have shaped it through the years, plus the meaningful nuances that later years added. Delbert McClinton sounds more soul than country, but he hit country's top ten in a 1993 duet with Tanya Tucker, country's bona fide wild-child woman. Some claim that Billy Ray Cyrus comes off more rock than country because his "Achy Breaky Heart" made him a superstar while painting him into the corner with a single brush and a single color. But Billy Ray later released one of the best songs ever recorded in Nashville, "When I'm Gone."

The former "Hillbilly Cat," Elvis Presley, blurred those boundaries between country and rock half a century ago. The King of Rock 'n' Roll scored with 84 country chart songs, including his first releases on the Sun Records label. He enjoyed 11 country number ones and led a rockabilly rebellion that gave country music some of its major stars—Johnny Cash, Jerry Lee Lewis, Carl Perkins and Charlie Rich.

Western swing kings like Bob Wills and his Texas Playboys lured George Strait into his big-band fascination, but Strait surprised me when I asked about his all-time favorite song.

"Merle Haggard has been such a big influence on my career," George answered. "I respect the things he's done for country music. 'Okie From Muskogee' is the song that grabbed hold of me and jerked me toward country music. That was the one. And Merle is the one who led me to Bob Wills and his Texas Playboys with the album *Best Damn Fiddle Player in the World.*"

Like the planets circling the sun, country music spins in cyclical patterns. For every *Urban Cowboy* craze, there's a George Strait, Ricky Skaggs or Randy Travis to take country music back to its roots, back to reality. For every head-line proclaiming doom and gloom for country music, there are forthcoming stories about its renaissance and resurgence in popularity. One generation spawns another.

When George Strait passes the baton, there are new talents who will love and respect the values that made Strait a country legend. Mark Chesnutt admires the way that the family-oriented George cut down his former demanding schedule of more than 200 concert dates a year to 70 or below. He loves the way Strait has maintained his private life without losing his fans.

Mark Chesnutt
(© Sony Music Entertainment Inc.)

"George has got it all," Mark praised. "He works only 50 to 60 dates a year, plays only the biggest venues in the best markets. Goes home. Goes fishing. Goes hunting. Does what he wants to do."

Mark contemplated the Strait life and added, "Eventually I want to be doing what he's doing."

And now, younger stars than Chesnutt appreciate the way he tries to aim his career in the direction he desires—to the top with less wear and tear from too many road dates.

Tom T. Hall Defines Country to a "T"

Tom T. Hall, one of the most gifted storytellers to emerge from the hills, offered a definition that fits the wide and wonderful world of country music. His 1974 number-one hit, "Country Is," remains as all-encompassing and relevant today as it did more than a quarter century ago:

"Country is…sitting on the back porch
Listening to the whippoorwill, late in the day.
Country is…minding your business
Helping a stranger, if he comes your way.
Country is…living in the city
Knowing your people, knowing your kind.
Country is…what you make it
Country is…all in your mind."

Basically, that's what country is. Country music aficionados do not need to live in the country. They can survive in style in the city. They can mind their own business or help a neighbor. As Tom T. Hall continues to explain in the song, country fans tend to love their towns, whether large or small, teach the children well, stand up for what's right, work hard and play hard.

Whether it's linked with the twang of guitars, the sweet sound of a mandolin, a rock 'n' roll beat, a reggae riff or gilded by a symphonic orchestra, country has become the music of the masses. And it fits that role well.

Simply stated, country music is—as Tom T. Hall sings— all in your mind, all in your heart.

Chapter 6

Waltzing Across Texas with Willie

On the Road Again

The minstrel of country music stays on the move, happy as a songbird on the wing when he's flying down the highways, restless as a caged cat when he's off the path, never at home on the range, always at home on the stage.

One of my favorite journeys on the long and winding road of country music was a two-day Texas trip with Willie Nelson. Odysseus, who took a decade to meander home after the Trojan War, has a modern-day wanderlusting soulmate in Willie.

On this bright, blue-sky morning, Nelson's perpetual motion propelled him from an Evergreen, Colorado, mountain retreat back to his beloved Lone Star state. The red-eye early-morning flight lifted him from Denver to Dallas, where we met up and hopped aboard Texas International Airlines, bound for Beaumont.

On the road again with Willie Nelson, Gerry Wood
presents the red-headed stranger with two Billboard *awards.*
(Photo courtesy of Gerry Wood)

A beautiful flight attendant smothered Willie with cof-
fee-tea-or-me attention as though Prince Charles had just
snuggled down into his royal first-class seat.

"Orange juice, please," he requested in that unmistak-
able granulated voice that graces his songs and conversa-
tions.

Seconds later the juice arrived…on a tray with the
stewardess's home address, phone number, probably her mea-
surements, and a request for an autograph. The soul-man
of country music quickly obliged.

"Hey, man, we enjoy your music," praised a passenger
seated in the row across from Willie.

"Thanks," Nelson replied, loving it when his music traverses the bridges of races, decades and genres—from past to present, from country to jazz, pop, blues, folk, rock and beyond. The countriest of all performers now performs for all countries, sliding in and out of styles with a versatile ease that's both fluid and fascinating.

As the airplane hurtled off the runway, Willie glanced out the window at the rapidly disappearing Dallas-Fort Worth Airport. "This is where I wrote 'Bloody Mary Morning,'" he informed me, the first fact in a trivia-packed informational tour.

No Bloody Marys this morning for Willie, though. Just another orange juice as the jet soared over the state where he reigns as musical monarch.

Sweet Memories in Beaumont

Texas International glided to a stop on the Beaumont airport tarmac and the passengers scrambled toward the terminal. Willie carried off his bag—a Texas hero gaining greetings, gawks and stares from his fellow travelers. The blazing sun seared down as he walked through the parking lot where a Mercedes-Benz had been deposited for his arrival.

Willie slipped behind the wheel for the trip downtown as the station on the radio hawked his upcoming concert. "Willie Nelson will be arriving in Beaumont before long for his sold-out show tonight," advised the slightly-behind-the-times deejay in resonant authoritative tones. "Now here's a Willie Nelson hit—'Sweet Memories.'"

As the song serenaded the airwaves, Willie kept one hand on the steering wheel and the other on the radio, cranking up the volume and concentrating on the soft and sensuous sound. "I love to hear my songs on the radio or jukebox to study what I did right or wrong," he explained. Not an exercise in ego-tripping, it's a case study of a creator seeking to improve his artistry, years after the recording was made, with the objectivity bestowed by the passage of time.

The car veered into the Red Carpet Inn parking lot, the afternoon sun still bearing down with relentless Texas persistence. The road crew had greased the skids for Willie's arrival with an advance check-in, so he picked up a key at the front desk and headed straight for his room, where he unpacked, donned running duds, and, thirteen minutes after arrival, bolted from the room for a jog.

Running Into and From Temptation

With traffic whizzing by, Willie sprinted along the highway before discovering a trail traversing through a middle-class neighborhood. After the second mile of this impromptu jog, a car passed, then screeched to a sudden stop, the tires burning rubber in the emergency. A blond woman poked her head out the window and marveled, "I just can't believe this! You're Willie Nelson, aren't you?"

His forehead beaded with sweat and his face gaining a crimson hue, Willie nodded in affirmation, enjoying the opportunity for a quick breather.

"My friends are not going to believe this at all!" she gushed. "They'll think I'm lying. But if I'm lying, I'm dying!"

"Are you coming to my show tonight?" Willie asked with a smile.

"No," she answered, as disappointment dimmed her enthusiasm. "I tried to get tickets, but they're all sold out."

"Tell me your name and we'll put you on the backstage list," he promised.

Her eyes ballooned to the size of a Texas full moon. "Oh, Lord, really?"

She provided her name to the most famous runner in Texas, and the wily Willie jogged on.

Soon, another would-be athlete appeared out of nowhere to join us. Texas-Moon Eyes had corralled a friend with a bulletin about the star sprinter gracing the steamy local pavement with his running shoes. Quickly caught up in the excitement of the moment, the winsome woman kept pace with us, even though her bare feet scooted perilously over pebbles, stones and occasional glass fragments. She would have walked over hot coals for this opportunity. The workout finally took us on a diversionary course to the nearby apartment of Texas-Moon Eyes and Barefoot Beauty.

Texas hospitality never looked better as the gorgeous flare-cheeked Temptation Twins offered us a break for ice water and no telling what else. But Willie's mind was on running, and after one glass of water we were off. On the road again, pounding the pavement, burning calories, sweating bullets, pumping more blood into the vessels and heart while escaping the afternoon delights that would have been forthcoming back at the apartment.

Beast, Snake and Happy Tripping

The jog ended where it started at the Red Carpet Inn. After a quick shower, Willie's running outfit gave way to jeans, T-shirt and a red and black bandana, his favorite attire for stage and life. After welcoming his Nashville songwriting buddy Hank Cochran for a chat about old times, show time neared and it was back to the car and the drive to the Beaumont Civic Center. A weird mixture of superstar and chauffeur, Willie drove himself to the backstage entrance.

First chore was to check on the three buses—one for the crew, another for the band, and the "Chuck Truck," the food-on-wheels bus bossed by a burly chef with the fitting name of Beast. The spicy aromas wafted with enticing intensity in Beast's kitchen, but Nelson moved on to the more worrisome crew bus. The straggling road survivors, in varied states of mental and physical disarray, were surviving their latest endless swing through America. That's all that their boss, Mr. Nelson, could request for the tattered tail end of a long expedition.

Willie then checked the band bus, the most vulnerable of the vehicles because of a popular gift. Some compassionate fans had dropped off a gallon jug of moonshine, a vile concoction of thick liquid, churned red and bloated with fleshy fat cherries that languished on the bottom in a gray rot. The jar had already taken a major hit, and the mood in the bus was downright congenial.

Everyone seemed to be having a good time—maybe too good—so Willie ventured over to Leon Russell's bus, greeting his friend who would be opening the show for him.

"Hi, Leon."

"Hi, Willie."

That ended the informalities. Leon wasn't conversing much in lucid terms these days, but he and Willie communicate on advanced levels where words are irrelevant. All is well in both worlds for these musicnauts blazing melodic trails through their private cosmos of time and space.

Willie's mind focused back on that ominous, and fast disappearing, moonshine supply. Instinctively recognizing any potential danger areas, he returned to the band bus, its destination sign above the front windshield reading HAPPY TRIPPING. This was a more serious visit than his previous "Hi, how're you doing?" appearance a few moments earlier. These guys would be backing him up onstage in just a few minutes, so they read a silent, somber warning in Willie's intense game face: perform now, play later. Without a word spoken, a band member quickly stashed the moonshine bottle into a cabinet where it would stay until the show finale.

Chris Ethridge, the bass player, typified the bond between Nelson and his band.

"Since I've been working for Willie," Chris told me, "I've already met my two idols—George Jones and President Jimmy Carter."

Willie absorbed the statement, looked Chris in the eyes and informed him, "Stick with me, kid, and you'll be wearing horse turds as big as diamonds."

Though the moonshine is history, the aroma of burning hemp filtered through the luxury bus. Snake, the road manager, poked his head through the mind-altering haze and announced, "You've got 15 minutes."

Willie utilized those 15 minutes and added another dozen to autograph a stack of posters.

Suddenly, Snake flashed Willie a cue, and Nelson beelined to the stage as 8,000 fans jumped to their feet in a standing ovation when he entered the spotlight.

Whiskey River Revisited

At 9:32 p.m. on a muggy night with the humidity higher than the temperature, "Whiskey River," Willie's standard show opener and closer, served its first purpose. A surge of thunderous applause, screams and shouts washed across the crowd like an audio tidal wave. The magic elixir of that sound flooded onto the stage, engulfing Nelson and his musicians, washing away troubles, exhaustion and the petty tribulations that stemmed from merging too many men too close together for too many days and nights on the road. The applause cleansed the past and provided a jolt of energy that would power the band and singer for the next two hours as they received as much as they gave.

Willie resurrected "Funny How Time Slips Away" from the dark ages of his Nashville past and followed it with a remarkable series of masterfully crafted compositions from his glory days as a songwriter—"Crazy," "Nightlife" and "Sweet Memories."

After a solid hour of hit after hit, he took a break and the spotlight beamed down on the white-whiskered space cadet wearing a cowboy hat. Leon Russell had been in the background innocuously playing keyboards on the side of the stage. But now center stage became his turf, and he took full advantage of the opportunity with a montage of his hits.

While Leon bared his creative soul, Nelson faced a backstage area full of mandatory duties. A photo to sign here, an autograph on the album cover there, a handshake with a radio program director, and several "you probably don't remember me, but..." introductions. Willie heard the cheering for his friend Leon and desperately wanted to watch the stirring show, but he couldn't, trapped by his own popularity.

Back to the Front

Nelson escaped the melee just in time to catch the last verse of Leon Russell's masterpiece "Lady Blue." Looking like a stoned Sphinx, Leon rocked the lyrics, pounded the keyboards and roused the fans.

After Russell's wife, Mary, belted out a stirring gospel number, Willie recaptured the stage and, with the show heating up along with the performers and audience, grabbed a Lone Star beer from the hands of the ever-present Snake. Shouts of audience approval accompanied the pop of the beer top. Despite Willie's reputation as a connoisseur of beer and marijuana, this was his first beer of the long day. He subsisted on orange juice, water and Texsun pink grapefruit juice before Lone Star entered his liquid diet mix.

"Blue skies, nothing but blue skies...." Willie refurbished a golden oldie, gilding it with his own bluesy style and unique pace and phrasing. He milked the mystery and nostalgia of the original version while implanting a totally new feel for the lyrics, meaning and melody. When the song ended, and before the applause withered, he segued straight into "Georgia On My Mind," another evergreen that gained new life with his masterful treatment.

He tried to close the show with "Will the Circle be Unbroken" and "Amazing Grace," but the crowd wouldn't let him off that easily. Deafening applause, whistles and rhythmic shouts drew him back to the stage after he walked off. Audience dreams turned into reality as Willie brought Leon along for an encore. Together they tore into "Luckenbach Texas" that gained a new lyric when Willie adlibbed, "Let's go to Luckenbach, Texas, with Willie and *Leon* and the boys...." Substituting the night's enchanted name of "Leon" for "Waylon" again brought the crowd to a fever pitch of excitement.

One more refrain of "Whiskey River" sailed Willie's stage day into home port, but not his night.

A dash for backstage brought him to a mélange of laminated-pass recipients, including the wildly applauding Texas-Moon Eyes. Her presence demonstrated once again the honesty and integrity of Willie Nelson. Despite the distractions and diversions of the day, he had somehow remembered to give her name to Snake, who put her on the VIP list.

No rest for a tired Willie. He graciously plodded through a radio interview and a slow pilgrimage among fans, posing for more photos, signing more autographs and dealing with the barrage of banal small talk from those who were too excited with the in-person experience to control their normal conversational thought processes.

Finally, near midnight, the exhausted entertainer collapsed into the welcome calm and quietude of the car for the journey back to the motel.

After the night wore down and the rush of the concert wore off, Willie managed to catch some sleep before arising for another day, another opening, another show, another highway to travel.

Whatever Happened to Ol' Willie?

Like his late friend Roger Miller, Willie Nelson has been known to stay awake for a day or three, but he works best on a solid eight hours sleep. He rose in time to bid goodbye and safe journey to the boys in the band bus, HAPPY TRIPPING. Last night's moonshine had taken its toll, leaving in its wake a cargo of hungover, groaning, not-so-happy trippers as the bus headed toward Austin.

Willie Nelson
(© Lost Highway)

Willie invited me to make the trek with him in the car, a short five-hour asphalt waltz across Texas to the state capitol, his home, and his next show.

"If we get to my house in time, we'll have time for a run," Willie promised, putting pedal to the metal.

As a driver, Willie Nelson makes a damn good singer. His heavy Texas foot accelerated the vehicle into a spastic spectrum of speed, from a lackadaisical 55 miles per hour to a stomach-wrenching 95. During the high-speed segments, my mind envisioned the next-day headlines in the *Austin Chronicle* and other newspapers across the globe: WILLIE NELSON AND SOMEONE ELSE DIE IN TEXAS CAR CRASH.

The radio slid across a wide range of music as Willie punched the buttons, finally settling on a country station. Later, a pit stop at a self-serve gas station offered the unexpected sight of this renowned artist pumping his own gas into the thirsty Mercedes. Midway on the journey, we paused at a ramshackle greasy-spoon roadside restaurant. Willie ordered a cheeseburger, fries and a Lone Star beer. Then he threw some quarters into the jukebox, selecting some past Willie Nelson hits.

"Aha," I joked, "can't get enough of your own music, huh?"

Not knowing if I were kidding or not, Willie took pains to explain. "No, I recorded this a long time ago and I just want to see if it still holds up after all these years."

Damn, I thought, this guy never stops.

After the cheeseburgers and beer became gastronomical history, it was back on the road again. The flatlands of Texas flew by and we passed an old two-story wooden farmhouse, set back from the highway and surrounded by giant shade trees. Willie pointed to the rural slice of Americana—the home with its front porch swing and the horses and cows grazing in the green-brown meadow near the barn.

"Now that's where I could be very happy." A wishful, wistful aura mellowed his voice. "Just hanging out on that porch on that swing. Looking at the beauty in the day, and at the stars at night. I'll just drop out and everybody will ask, 'I wonder whatever happened to Ol' Willie?'"

I realized I had just discovered the essence of Willie Nelson. And it was consistent with every aspect of his character that I had ever known. He handles whatever life throws his way with peace and serenity whether it's the adulation of thousands of fans in the frenzy of a concert or the soul-nurturing sensation of sitting alone on a porch swing in wondrous contemplation of, and communication with, the star-studded heavens until, as Hank Williams sang, "the silence of a falling star lights up a purple sky."

Like that falling star, the rest of our trip was in silence.

No Key for His Castle

The electronic gate at the 44-acre ranch swung open at the press of a button in the car. Willie drove past the tall stone fence that guarded the property from those who forced him to erect it. He parked in the driveway, walked to the front door of the large house and inserted a key. It didn't work. He tried another. And another. The lock didn't budge.

"I might not have the right keys," he said calmly.

By now, I would have been smashing windows, shattering doors or whatever it took to get into my own home, knowing I had a few bucks left to repair my patience-deprived damage.

But not Willie. He displayed no signs of irritation to a happening that would have sent lesser mortals up the wall. He tried the keys in a back door with similar results.

"A million-dollar house and you can't get in," I prodded him. "Back when you lived in Nashville and didn't have any money, I bet you had no trouble getting in your house."

"Yes," Willie agreed with a wry smile, recalling his wild and woolly Nashville days. One time he came home drunk and passed out on the bed, and his angry wife wreaked revenge by pulling the bed sheets over him and sewing him within them like a cocoon. His bleary, hangover awakening the next morning, red eyes crying in the reign of all-encompassing sheets, must have been disorienting if not traumatic.

I realized that an intellectual or philosophical discourse with Willie would be like taking on Buddha, so I let the subject drop.

"We'll just change for running out here in the driveway," he said, solving the first problem of where to change clothes. He'd let the key problem solve itself later.

On the Run with Willie

The car trunk reinvented itself as our dressing room as we stripped and adorned shorts, T-shirts and jogging shoes.

Then came miles of running up to the front gate, back down a trail to a waterfall at the far end of his property, back to the gate, back to the waterfall, multiplied several times.

Part of the run was conversational between us:

"Willie, what's it like to run through the snow in Colorado?"

"Gerry, it was great—so peaceful. Probably like what you were telling me about the time you ran ten miles along the ocean in Old Orchard Beach, Maine."

Silence dominated another part of the run. Total meditation, arms flung out, measured bursts of breathing, body and mind on cruise control. A time to cleanse and renew flesh and soul, as Willie purged yesterday's excesses, contemplated today's and prepared for tomorrow's.

Before we dashed the last half-mile, a pickup truck made its dusty way down the driveway and stopped next to us. The driver, Willie's son-in-law, had learned about the lockout and dashed off for a key. When the exercise portion of our day ended at sunset, the door to the Nelson manse was keyed open and a welcomed, nourishing shower followed.

Willie's daughter dropped by for some private family talk with her father. In the den, Willie sank into the comfortable embrace of a chair, simultaneously enjoying and combating the tranquility of these rare domestic moments with his daughter, granddaughter and son-in-law.

Another poignant discovery revealed Willie's absolute and uncompromising commitment to life on the road instead of the soothing ease of decent dwellings and fine family.

As he absorbed the love and the ambiance, he turned to me and confided, "It wouldn't do for me to live here. I'd mellow out and just stay here."

"The comfort of this safe place compared to the trauma of your traveling trail," I said. "Doesn't it make you just want to stay here?"

"Yes," he confessed, his expression hinting that he might have been caught in a weak moment. "After every tour, I swear it'll be my last one. But after I'm home for a couple days, I'm ready to go back on the road."

That explains the redheaded stranger's addiction to white lights and blue highways.

The brief respite at the ranch has lasted less than two hours. And now this most valiant of road warriors craved another mainline shot of stage adrenaline. He couldn't get it here at home because the cabinets were empty of that drug. The journey junkie was drawn back to the glaring white heat of the spotlight like a moth to the flame. He craved making music with his friends. He craved the highway ahead and where it led.

Goodbyes, hugs, kisses, all rendered with heartfelt love, and Willie Nelson was on the road again.

Winning the Battle of Waterloo

The car radio blasted the live broadcast of Austin's Waterloo Festival as Nelson maneuvered to the backstage gate entrance.

The headlights swept over and illuminated a human zoo inhabited by a funky menagerie caged behind gates and fences. Roaming the zoo were gorilla-like security guards, furry-brained happy-tripping band mates, crew members moving with gazelle speed, an ant swarm of media, goat-nervous managers and agents, shark-frenzied lawyers, tumblebug publicists, magpie-mouthed radio deejays, fine-feathered city officials strutting with peacock pride, star-thirsty groupies with the sexual morals of monkeys, and eagle-eyed, wary police wondering what to make of this mess. And, of course, there was Snake and Beast.

All awaited the highly anticipated arrival of the night's headline act, Willie Nelson. And all, in one way or another, wanted a piece of him.

Behind the steering wheel, Willie took it all in and then took a deep breath and exhaled a sigh. The serene day behind him contrasted dramatically with the spectacle that lay ahead. His eyes grew suddenly weary.

He veered away quickly from the gate, almost scraping it during a sharp U-turn.

For once, the moth had escaped the flame. Back on the road and the freedom it always brought him, Willie said, "Well, we're not quite ready for 'Whiskey River' yet. Let's go get a beer."

We landed at the Backstage, a spacious Austin establishment owned by proprietor Willie Nelson. He ordered coffee. I asked for a Lone Star beer. Flashbacks of the venue mob prompted Willie to alter his request. "I'll have a Lone Star, too," he told the waitress.

A business partner arrived at the table, and their discussion turned to profits, losses, taxes, money earned, money lost, and a deal involving 13 acres in Austin. Not quite the picture those fans back at the festival might project about Willie's life, and not quite the picture that Willie enjoys.

A trip back to the zoo started to look more alluring than this boring walk through decimal points. Willie checked his watch to end the conversation that drained him. Time had flown once again. Running late, he departed Backstage for backstage without finishing his beer.

When we returned to Waterloo Park, the multitude was smoking whatever grass wasn't being sat upon.

The déjà vu blues, all over again. He visited the band bus where the musicians were listening to tapes of the soon-to-be-released Willie Nelson/Leon Russell duet album. By now, the seconds, minutes, hours, days, nights, months, years and 24-hour cycles have blurred into a timeless warp zone.

The haze fogged memories of where was the last show? The last meal? The last recording session? The last phone call to friends? The last quality time spent at home with family and memories?

The only constant, the only touchstone with reality in this unreal existence, was making music.

And it was time to do that now.

At 11 p.m. in Austin, Texas, Willie Nelson took the stage to a standing ovation.

"Whiskey River take my mind..." he sang. The crowd of 15,000 erupted. He absorbed the energy and love generated by the audience reaction, and a familiar, knowing smile mellowed his weathered face, as wrinkled as a roadmap.

This time he was ready for "Whiskey River."

The Nightlife is the Right Life

The Waterloo Festival performance evolved into another magical, mystical night that Willie needs and deserves for his concerts, for his life. The balmy humid breeze, the devoted audience and the sounds from the stage all formed a powerful trilogy as the beat went on, the music supplied by a good man with a good heart and a good soul.

"The nightlife ain't no good life, but it's my life," Willie sang, an autobiographical verse if there ever was one.

The consummate country artist adopted the nightlife with all its inherent pleasures and pains. He crafted it to encompass his own lifestyle until it has become his existence, his family and his fortune.

For Willie Nelson, the nightlife ain't no bad life, after all.

Chapter 7

Country Women on Top

You Go, Girls!

From the days of the distaff side of the Carter Family to the Kitty Wells combative answer song "It Wasn't God Who Made Honkytonk Angels," to Loretta Lynn's brash ball-busting threat "Don't Come Home A-Drinkin' (With Lovin' On Your Mind)," women have always made their mark on country music.

Yet country remained male-dominated into the 1990s. Men controlled the creative process as well as, ironically, the purse strings. But as Bob Dylan once musically observed, the times, they are a-changing.

It wasn't an easy battle. For many years, women sat in the back of the country music bus. No matter how hard they worked, how grand their accomplishments, how much talent they demonstrated, they still went into the studios with male producers who often dictated what to sing and how to sing it. Often the songs just happened to be written or published by those producers—a lucrative side business. Women were subjects of a system rigged with more restrictive walls than a death row cell—thick, menacing and uncompromising.

"Women had been told what to do, but now we're thinking for ourselves," Reba McEntire said during a meeting in the plush offices of her own Starstruck Entertainment corporate empire. "We are now listening to our hearts and our gut instincts. We're not going to quit, either. We're going to keep on at it."

The impressive Starstruck building in Nashville's Music Row area stands as a monument to Reba's conviction, commercial creativity and business acumen. The rodeo-riding redhead from Oklahoma has forged a multifaceted career in music, movies, network television and as an acclaimed actress on New York City's Broadway.

Along with Reba, the hottest country touring acts of recent vintage include Shania Twain, Faith Hill, and the Dixie Chicks, even after Natalie Maines plunged the group into hot chicken soup during the 2003 conflict in Iraq. The Texas-based Chick told a London concert audience, "Just so you know, we're ashamed the President of the United States is from Texas." Natalie later apologized, but many angry Chicks fans flew the coop, never to return.

After a sluggish and lackluster start with her first releases, Shania Twain finally burst through the barriers with her appropriately titled album *The Woman In Me*. Crammed with hits, it gained quadruple platinum certification (more than four million sold) only ten months after its release—the fastest certified album in history for a woman artist. The gorgeous Canada-born chanteuse turned that breakthrough album into a launching pad for phenomenal acclaim. Twain evolved into a true international star, capable of dazzling a global audience with her high-energy halftime performance at the 2003 Super Bowl extravaganza in San Diego while racking up astonishing pop and country album sales and concert grosses.

With chart and concert success comes power...and control. Pam Tillis became one of the first female country talents to produce her own albums. An increasing number of women now share production duties with male producers or are taking full charge in the studio. Meanwhile, Tillis, Lorrie Morgan and Carlene Carter landed the blue-ribbon sponsor, Kraft Foods, for the first major all-female concert swing in country music. Four more stunning talents—Martina McBride, Mary Chapin Carpenter, Trisha Yearwood and Kim Richey—spearheaded another notable all-woman tour.

During one grand moment, Faith Hill, Shania Twain and Terri Clark captured the top three spots on *Billboard's* Hot Country Singles & Tracks chart. Close behind were Reba McEntire, Martina McBride, Patty Loveless, Linda Davis, Pam Tillis, Lorrie Morgan and Lari White. Then Twain leapfrogged both Garth Brooks and Alan Jackson when she jumped to No. 1 on the album chart. Vaulting out of nowhere to win four Country Music Association awards the first year she was nominated, bluegrass virtuoso Alison Krauss wowed critics and fans alike with her heaven-sent, sweet, wisp of a voice.

Cold Hands, Warm Heart

The times have changed for Reba—performer, wife and mother. How entertainers like her, Wynonna Judd, Martina McBride, Shania Twain and Faith Hill can maintain demanding, exhausting and time-consuming careers while tending to endless family chores remains one of the great mysteries of country music. It might have something to do with the eternal blessings and power of motherhood that tap deep into the nourishing wellsprings of love and energy.

Or maybe it's the comfortable foundation of family and home that helps offset the formidable rigors of the road. Between recording sessions, video shoots and concerts, McEntire returned home exhausted one frosty February day. But during an interview a few hours later, she was relaxed and renewed, laughing about her son Shelby, then eight years old. After playing outside in the bitter winter cold, he ran into the house, rubbing his frigid red hands together briskly. "Mom," complained Shelby, "my hands! They're freezing their butts off!"

Mother Reba had to stifle laughter as she scolded Shelby about his language. When she quizzed him about where he heard the B-word, Shelby took the juvenile version of the Fifth Amendment. "I think," Reba confided, "that Shelby got it from Jones, the bus driver. But Jones says it wasn't him."

Hill Keeps the Faith

Faith Hill credits husband Tim McGraw with helping her raise their three daughters. "I lean on him a lot," she said. Rather than allowing her ever-expanding professional career to rule her life, Faith turns her focus toward her young children. "Instead of worrying about myself and my career," she said, "I worry about Gracie, Maggie and Audrey. They are the main concern for both Tim and me. I'm so blessed to have my career and my family, too. It keeps my feet firmly on the ground."

Hill mixes music biz with family biz by bouncing her newly recorded songs off her oldest daughters for their reaction. She receives honest responses from her five and four year olds, Gracie and Maggie. When they like it, they sing along. When they don't, they tell her why. Audrey, the youngest, hasn't joined the chorus of critics yet, but she'll be there in a few years, Faith promised.

Follow the Leaders

Lari White credits trailblazing predecessors Loretta Lynn and Tammy Wynette for her own career climb that resulted in a gold record. "They opened a lot of doors," White noted. "Loretta and Tammy paved the way for people like me— young female artists—to really have a lot more strength and a lot more independence."

The remarkable *Trio* album bonded Dolly Parton, Emmylou Harris and Linda Ronstadt into a soulful sisterhood and reshaped Lari's perception of what talented, driven, determined, dynamic women can accomplish.

"When they did that album," Lari related, "I listened closely to it, over and over. And then I was like: This is *my* album! Three of my favorite people on one record—and just listen to what they are writing and singing!'"

White exhibits an uncanny ability to choose the best role models for a rising female performer. They don't come better than Dolly Parton, Emmylou Harris, Linda Ronstadt, Loretta Lynn and Tammy Wynette.

Dolly Parton Zings Porter Wagoner

An east Tennessee mountain spirit, Dolly Parton rode her ebullient personality and superb songwriting and singing skills to the highest realms of the entertainment world. Meanwhile she built a vast business and charity empire involving records, music publishing, TV shows, movies, merchandising and the Dollywood theme park, one of Tennessee's top attractions. She has inspired countless hopefuls with her energy and fortitude and could charm a snake from the bushes with her straightforward, sometimes self-deprecating, sense of humor.

During a Nashville music business roast for her former mentor and duet partner Porter Wagoner, Dolly's wit both sparkled and spanked. Although Wagoner helped guide Parton to fame early in her career, business quarrels and personal clashes divided them as she zoomed to celebrity status. Despite the past friction, Dolly delivered some compliments at the event. But the impish artist couldn't resist referring to Wagoner's rumored sexual escapades with several country stars, including herself.

"One time, Jeannie Seely and Tammy Wynettte came to me real concerned," related Dolly. "They were worried about a rumor going around that Porter was saying he had slept with all of us. They wondered what we should do about that rumor. I told Jeannie and Tammy, 'Don't worry about this, girls, because half of the people will think Porter is lying, and the other half will think we've got bad taste.'"

As the room rocked with laughter, Porter Wagoner was speechless…because he was laughing, too.

Dolly had done it again.

*Dolly Parton with Key West author Carol Shaughnessy and Gerry Wood in 1990.
(Photo courtesy of Gerry Wood)*

A Stellar Performance by Stella

Another member of the Parton clan has also won hard-
earned fame as a singer, actress and songwriter. Stella Parton, Dolly's younger sister, struggled valiantly to emerge from
the blanket of her superstar sister's shadow. She has succeeded in many ways.

Stella has written and performed her way into the top
echelon of the country music charts, acted in movies and

off-Broadway touring shows and stays busy with concerts, writing books and marketing her impressive catalog of CDs that range from Appalachian country roots music to gospel and bluegrass. Stella's first single, "I Want To Hold You In My Dreams Tonight," soared all the way into *Billboard's* Top Ten, notifying the world that the deep Parton talent gene pool goes far beyond one person.

Winner of the 2002 Christian Country Music Association Mainstream Country Artist Award, Stella recalls the early exploitive expectations of the media when a new breed of beautiful young country stars burst onto the scene. TV shows and publications suddenly came calling for the hot new artist, including the men's magazine *Oui*, requesting an interview and photo session. Actually, *Oui* desired nude photos more than naked words.

In her twenties at the time, Stella was in for a shock. "I was still pretty naïve about things," she told me years later. "I had no idea what kind of publication *Oui* was. I thought it was like *People* or *Us*. I didn't know French or its pronunciation, so I figured it was *We*, a competitor to *Us*. It made a lot of sense to me—just another family magazine."

Stella discovered a new definition for family when she arrived at the photo session in Los Angeles. This family was more like Ozzy Osbourne's than Ozzie Nelson's! She entered the makeup room where a few scanty nighties were laid out in a corner.

"There wasn't a rack of clothes for me—just some crotchless panties and lacy corsets that looked like they were exhibits from an adult bookstore raid. I said, 'Where are my clothes?'"

"What clothes?" they asked.

Stella picked up the panties with a finger and thumb as though they were contaminated. "This is just underwear!"

Stella Parton and Gerry Wood celebrate Stella's new CD release, Appalachian Blues.
(Photo courtesy of Gerry Wood)

After winning an intense battle for more Stella-friendly fashions, she encountered the photographer, famed for his clothes-challenged layouts for *Playboy* and other magazines known more for their revealing flashes of female flesh than for intellectual articles. "He was upset because I wouldn't get naked for him and his camera," Stella said. "I wouldn't wear those things they laid out for me. I finally wore some lacy anklets, tight satin shorts and a pink tank top."

So why didn't Stella take it all off like so many stars before her?

"I didn't want to disappoint my mom and dad and break their hearts," she explained. "Also, I'm very shy, so I wouldn't have done it anyway."

But she learned why some stars bare their flesh for the cameras.

"When I saw all the food, champagne and other enticements they had available, and they got through telling me how gorgeous I was and how I should share that beauty with the world, I could see why some of those girls stripped."

The photographer was relentless and angry. "What is it with all you Southern country women?" he demanded.

Feisty Stella fought back. "I've got a dad and five brothers at home, and there's no way I could go back if I got naked and those pictures showed up in your magazine."

The photographer huffed and hissed, unconvinced.

"You wouldn't want to deal with them if they saw that," Stella warned. "They are all as mean as those guys in that movie *Deliverance*. You don't want them after you—know what I mean?"

The photographer, who apparently had seen the movie, got the message, and Stella got her way, saying "Non" to *Oui*, as she learned her first few words of French the hard way.

Women Better Be Best

Moving beyond songs just about lost love and romance gone astray, ladies are tackling tough issues like never before. Mary Chapin Carpenter cut to the quick of male-dominated, one-sided relationships with her lancing lyrics in "He Thinks He'll Keep Her." Spawned from a 1950s-era TV commercial, the song skewers the chauvinistic arrogance of a husband who thinks he'll "keep" his wife because of her domestic prowess. K.T. Oslin wrote and recorded powerful statements such as her hit "'80s Ladies" that revealed the innermost feelings, hopes and fears of women. Reba McEntire dealt directly with the controversial topic of AIDS in the haunting and riveting "She Thinks His Name Was John." And Martina McBride, dramatizing a troubling tale written by Gretchen Peters, denounced domestic violence with "Independence Day."

Earning the freedom to excel in the board room as well as the studio, on the road as well as at home, these gifted artists will be role models for the next generation. Against daunting odds and resistance, they took control of their careers without shortchanging their families.

"We feel like we have to try harder and really stand out to break through as female artists," stated Lari White. "It's that minority mindset where it's not enough to just be as good as others. You've got to be better. In fact, you've got to be a *lot* better."

That philosophy, put to action, explains why the country acts performing in the coveted slot of Super Bowl entertainers in 2003 were all women—Shania Twain and the Texas trio of the Dixie Chicks.

They, and their superstar sisters, are the cream of the country music crop.

And, as the saying goes, the cream always rises to the top.

Chapter 8

Conway Don't Allow Nothin' on His Bus

The Gospel According to Porkchop

The first thin light of morning encouraged dawn to paint the horizon with broad strokes of dark red and purple hues as we loaded up the tour bus. This sleep-deprived entourage of musicians trudged aboard ready to aim south from Hendersonville, Tennessee, on a beeline to Ozark, Alabama, for a Conway Twitty concert with Loretta Lynn.

When the sky muted to blood red, I recalled the mariner's adage, "Red skies at night, sailor's delight. Red sky in the morning, sailor's warning." Although the nearest ocean was hundreds of miles away from inland Tennessee, nearby Old Hickory Lake cradled enough water and sailboats to render the advice, however diluted, relevant for this voyage.

We didn't have to wait long for the star of the show. Groggy and unshaven, Conway Twitty, tripping somewhere within the ethereal twilight zone of slumber and sense, headed straight for his master bedroom in the rear quarters. With nary a word to anyone, he closed the door, and that was the last we were to see of the former Harold Lloyd Jenkins for quite a while.

But it wasn't the last of the Twitty influence on the forward section that I shared with his band members and driver. The bus geared onto the road, seeking Interstate 65 South, and I reached into my carry-on bag for a pen and paper to duly chronicle the trip for a *Billboard* magazine special edition. Conway had ridden the rock 'n' roll rocket to the top of *Billboard's* pop chart on November 10, 1958, with the chord-scaling "It's Only Make Believe." Yet, like such other "rock" stars as Johnny Cash, Carl Perkins and Jerry Lee Lewis, he still dreamed of a country music career. Conway converted to country in the mid-60s, and the genre jump paid off in spades—more than 30 number-one solo hits and several more with Loretta Lynn. The unraveling drama of life on the road with a top country star should provide some interesting moments for our readers, I thought, as I steeled myself for a long, exhausting day and night of observations and interviews.

Eagle-eyed Porkchop Markham, Twitty's drummer, spotted me groping blindly through the endless caverns and crevices of my carry-on bag, dubbed, for good reason, "The Mixmaster." The alert musician assumed I was hand-hunting a pack of cigarettes. He moved across the aisle to the lounge seat beside me, a serious expression clouding his worried face.

"Gerry," Porkchop said. "You ain't smoking, are you?"

"No," I replied. "I don't smoke. Never have. Damn stuff will kill you."

"Good," he said, his face mellowing. "Conway don't allow no smoking on his bus."

Tall Cotton at the Carter White House: Left to right at a party honoring country music are Tennessee Senator Jim Sasser, Conway Twitty, President Jimmy Carter, Loretta Lynn, Tom T. Hall, Ed Shea, southern director of ASCAP, First Lady Rosalyn Carter and Gerry Wood, then southern editor of Billboard.
(Photo courtesy of Gerry Wood)

The Desert of Alabama

Tennessee morphed seamlessly into Alabama as we rolled at 77 miles per hour toward our destination. The sun-bleached landscape we sped through displayed little of value to a writer who was suddenly made thirsty gazing at the parched flatlands that glided past the dark tinted windows. I ventured to the mini-refrigerator in the lounge of the mini-kitchen, pulled open the mini-door and prayed for a maxi-Coke.

I got a Porkchop instead of a Coke. I felt a tap on my shoulder. I turned and saw his cherubic countenance evolve, before my very eyes, into wrinkles of worry.

"Gerry," Porkchop said. "You ain't drinking, are you?"

As the refrigerator revealed a variation on the theme of emptiness, I answered, "Apparently not. I gave up drinking this morning. I just like to check out empty refrigerators. It's a hobby of mine."

"Good," he said. "Conway don't allow no drinking on his bus."

Bye Bye Barbecue...Hello, Colonel Sanders

Noon became history. Conway remained secluded in his movable lair like the Pope in the papal chambers while my throat screamed for a beverage and my stomach joined the angry chorus with audible hunger-related moans for food.

Frequent sightings of ramshackle roadside barbecue joints severely aggravated my plight. Dirty, decrepit, run-down shacks with faded tin signs that depicted oddly happy pigs seconds away from their fate which for these porkers was definitely the pits, in more ways than one. Apparently, the soon-to-be-dispatched swine harbored death wishes since they waved and smiled while proclaiming the word that would kill them: BAR-B-QUE.

A veteran of youthful mutton-stalking trips to Woolfolk's Barbecue in Henderson, Kentucky, I knew that the world's best barbecue is not served in upscale establishments that require indoor plumbing. Woolfolk's fine diners knew the wisdom of visiting the outhouse *after* eating, and not before. But find a bug-infested, Hades-hot, hovel with walls thickened and darkened to a rich molasses shade by decades of dense, fat-dripping hickory smoke, then you've found a slice of paradise for the palate. Though I could not smell the wisps of smoke curling out of the chimneys, these godforsaken ptomaine palaces still teased me with their solid visual credentials. And I pined to dine at one of these wooden huts before it burned to the ground, a chronic problem due to the combustible combination of fire and wood and fat.

But the bus sped along, ignoring the carnivorous calling that besets most humans. All the happy pigs hawking their own flesh did not work with this driver.

Finally, at 1:47 p.m., the Conway cruiser slowed for an exit and pulled off the highway. I hoped for the best—a simple barbecue shack.

No way. We lurched toward a Kentucky Fried Chicken fast-foot eatery. Not that I have anything against fried chicken or Kentucky. I eat the former, grew up in the latter, and admired Colonel Sanders. But, no, *please*, not when there's barbecue within salivating distance. Barbecued road kill at that instant of famishment emerged as a viable option.

Conway's musicians scrambled off the bus in a hasty assault on the restaurant, trailed by the portly Porkchop, huffing behind his slimmer fellow travelers. Looking at those hefty haunches jiggling before me, I endured a brief cannibalistic truth: even Porkchop's name now teased my appetite.

Porkchop and pals beat me to the chow line, and by the time I was able to order, and receive, a chicken breast and drumstick, the driver barked out an immediate departure. Leaving now, he warned. Without a moment to taste a bite, I wrapped my meal in a napkin that surrendered to golden splotches of grease. Clutching my coveted chicken with the passion of one entrusted with possession of the Holy Grail, I raced to the bus, its motor revving in a sign of straggler impatience.

I regained my seat as we pulled away and hit I-65 again, the drone of the engines spewing their mesmerizing monotony along with their fumes. Almost visible in its intensity, the aroma of the chicken wafted up to my flared nostrils. The acute sense of smell relayed the information to my stomach that grudgingly mellowed in mood and promised me all would be forgiven and its bitching would cease as soon as I shoved some of this delight down the tubes. "But you'd better hurry," it growled at me. I scraped the soggy napkin from the sticky skin of the chicken, grabbed the drumstick, raised it in triumph to my watering mouth, and prepared to chomp down on my Alabama gourmet meal.

Porkchop approached. Not a good sign.

"Gerry," Porkchop said. "You ain't eating, are you?"

"No, Porkchop. I just brought this along because I collect chicken legs. It's another hobby of mine."

"Good," he said. "Conway don't allow no eating on his bus."

Relieved that I had no plans to violate Twitty Bus Rule number three, Porkchop, beamed apostolic approval and the wisdom of a modern day Moses hauling the heavy stone tablets of Conway's commandments down the highway of road life. With my previous three near-infractions, I would be pushing misdemeanor toward felony territory had it not been for his sharp eyes. Curiously he didn't seem preoccupied at all about my alleged hobbies, perhaps because they fell outside the realm of Twitty's golden rules.

With great regret, I stuffed the chicken down into the inner sanctums of my carry-on, scene of previous food-related mishaps involving a leaky plastic container of Vincent's Clam Bar pasta sauce from New York, the untimely spilling of a gallon jug of Texas barbecue sauce from the Iron Works BBQ in Austin and the pungent explosion of a Muffaleta sandwich from the Central Grocery in New Orleans. All the disasters, unfortunately, had taken place on airplanes, to my dismay and the discomfort of fellow passengers at the moment the fragrances permeated the re-circulated air, first class to the last row of coach.

No Privacy in the Privy

Pushed to the breaking point, I prepared to quiz Porkchop about what in the hell Conway *does* allow on his bus. But first I needed to rid my hands of Colonel Sanders' finger-lickin' grease, a painful reminder of the chicken I didn't have the pleasure of eating.

As I washed my hands in the bathroom sink, a strong knocking rattled the door, interrupting the cleansing process.

"Gerry. Gerry!"

The voice of Porkchop Markham. I knew it well.

"Yes, Porkchop, what is it now?"

"Gerry," Porkchop said. "You ain't shittin', are you?"

"I wouldn't dare, Porkchop." I was unable to quickly come up with any alleged hobby involving this particular body function. Over the roar and vibration of the engine, I heard a sigh of relief from the other side of the door.

"Good," he said. "Because Conway don't allow no shittin' on his bus."

A Country Music Hall
of Famer Comes to the Rescue

When commanded not to do something, my mind and body react with an unbridled powerful thrust in the opposite direction—an instant knee-jerk mechanism. Suddenly, I experienced a puzzling, yet overwhelming, urge to smoke a cigarette. I also craved a drink—a strong one. Rum preferably. Forget the mixer. I wanted to eat. Chicken. Barbecue. Porkchops.

Though I had no legitimate reason for this to happen because of the recent mandated absence of food from my diet, my body triggered signals to the side of the brain that notified me that I needed to defecate. A major sensory battle brewed internally between my organs and my brain, and I felt as though I were the neutral third party as these forces fought it out—something like the United States would feel if Canada declared war on Mexico.

At the approach of nightfall, we arrived in Ozark, Alabama. I felt so dry, so thirsty, so hungry, so deprived, when the chamber of horrors fumed its way to the auditorium backstage parking lot. Then, like a desert survivor crawling over a dune to discover an oasis, I spotted either a mirage or the Loretta Lynn tour bus. It turned out to be Loretta's bus.

"Bye, Porkchop, see you after the show," I said, bolting down the aisle before he had time to deliver one possible final "Hotel California" type of Conway decree: "Conway don't allow no *leaving* on his bus."

Like an escapee from a Stephen King novel, I fled the cage for Loretta's enticing heaven on wheels parked nearby.

I banged on the door to the Lynn luxury liner, realizing that these were fellow Kentuckians who would have many more "dos" and a lot less "don'ts" than the former Harold Lloyd Jenkins and his mobile dungeon.

The door opened with the majestic promise of the Pearly Gates.

And there, at the top of the steps, stood Ernest Rey, Loretta's son, grinning down at me. "Well, Gerry, what are you doing here?" he asked in a voice that sounded like gravel rolling down a washboard. Yet it was the sweetest sound I had ever heard.

"Escaping!" I gasped, my eyes begging for rescue.

"Well, come on in! Want a beer?"

I scrambled aboard the friendly confines. Ernest yanked a can of beer out of the refrigerator and handed it to me with a bowl of pretzels.

"Okay if I use your bathroom?"

"Sure. That's what it's here for."

Loretta emerged from her bedroom, still arranging her hair. "Well, hi, there," she greeted in her heartwarming country twang. "You down here for the show?"

"You bet, Loretta. Haven't seen you onstage for a long time."

"We're going back to Nashville right after the show if you want to ride back with us," she offered. "Excuse me, I've gotta get ready now." She pointed to her tousled coal black hair that screamed for major work before her onstage appearance in front of thousands of fans. "I'd scare 'em off for good, looking like this!"

Loretta disappeared back into the bedroom for final repairs.

"Ernest, thanks for the beer."

"Want another one, Gerry? How about a cigarette?"

"Thanks, I don't smo…" I halted before ending the sentence as Ernest reached into his shirt pocket for a pack of Winstons, flicked it open and offered me one.

"Sure, Ernest. Thanks a lot."

The window revealed, only a few yards away, the grim visage of the Twitty bus, looming as deceptive and dangerous as a Venus flytrap. Somehow I had sailed through the turbulent seas on Conway's land-barge with a safe arrival in the port of Ozark. Like Loretta, Conway had to be in his bedroom primping for the show. I didn't know exactly what he was doing—probably starching his hair—but I did know four things he *wasn't* doing. I shuddered at the thought of more miles with the master of road rules.

Then, in the Loretta Lynn bus in that dark, dank parking lot in the tiny town of Ozark, Alabama, while drinking a beer to chase a pretzel and fondling the cigarette in my hand, an incredible moment arrived.

I had an epiphany.

It jolted through me, toe to head, with the sudden shock and electrifying energy of a lightning bolt out of the black sky. The jagged message branded indelibly into the gray matter of my beleaguered, war-weary brain.

Thanks to the Book of Revelation of St. Porkchop the Large that offered a way into a monastic existence, and the Book of Exodus of Loretta the Great that offered a way out, the epiphany anointed me with an eternal truth:

There is a God.

Chapter 9

Tammy Wynette—
Country Soul Gone Too Soon

The First Lady of Country Music

The triumphant and tragic life and times of Tammy Wynette could fill several volumes of *Tales from Tammy* books. Born on May 5, 1942 in Itawamba County, Mississippi, Virginia Wynette Pugh worked as a Birmingham, Alabama, beautician before moving to Nashville to pursue a singing career in 1966.

Tammy ran into the perfect producer for her dramatically different voice and style. The legendary Billy Sherrill took her to the country music charts that same year with "Apartment #9." After her first chart single peaked at No. 44 on the *Billboard* country chart, the year of 1967 saw her breaking through as a major new star. "Your Good Girl's Gonna Go Bad" peaked at No. 3, and her next release, "My Elusive Dreams" soared to the top of the charts—the first

Tammy Wynette, the First Lady of Country Music, with Gerry Wood.
(Photo courtesy of Gerry Wood)

of 17 No. 1 solo records for the frail singer who battled health problems throughout most of her career.

A member of the Country Music Hall of Fame, Wynette won Country Music Association awards as top female vocalist in 1968, 1969 and 1970. Her soulful performances gave country music some of its most majestic musical moments. She scored with such heart-tugging ballads as "Stand By Your Man," "'Til I Get It Right" and "You And Me."

Tammy also tallied 13 Top 40 duet hits with George Jones, including three No. 1 smashes. Married to Jones from 1969 to 1975, Tammy and her singing partner spelled out the end of their marriage to the tune of her previous chart topping hit—"D-I-V-O-R-C-E." Three years later she married her manager George Richey, who was with her through her dying day of April 6, 1998.

Unfortunately, Tammy's death, at age 55, produced legal wrangling and a war of words that included some of her daughters, one of Wynette's doctors, and Richey. Stung by some of the criticisms leveled at him, George Richey offered me an exclusive interview to set the record straight from his point of view. As we sat down in the kitchen/den area of the Nashville home that he and the frequently hospitalized Tammy had shared, George responded to some of the accusations made against him in a book written by one of the daughters. Here's what he had to say.

Tammy's Last Hours

I think we all would want to look back and say was there something more I could have done for her that I didn't. I suppose that's part of the process of healing that I first went through—what could I have done differently, what could I do, what could I have done that maybe I didn't do?

The second part is that I was totally devoted to Tammy, but, then again, those who know me already know that's accurate.

In retrospect, no, I don't know what I could have done differently that would have made a better life for her. I did all that I knew to do.

That's not to say that I didn't make mistakes. In a relationship as long as we were together, who doesn't have faults? But I can tell you that my heart was always in the right place when it came to my wife. I adored her. I did everything that I knew to do for her. But her children, I believe, know that I did everything I could possibly do to better her life.

At the time of Tammy's death, I had been up for two days and nights because Tammy had a very tough weekend. During the day, we were napping on the couch in the kitchen. I recall hearing Tammy say several times to the housekeeper, "Please be quiet. Try to let him rest. He's had very little rest this weekend—he's been up with me all this weekend." That shows you the type of person Tammy was— she was the sick one, and she was worried about *me*.

I got a phone call at five minutes to seven Monday evening, April 6. It was my daughter in San Diego. When I woke up, I said to her, "I'll call you back in just a minute— I must run to the bathroom." I then noticed this note that was Scotch-taped to the glass top coffee table in the kitchen. It was from the housekeeper. It was posted at 6:05 p.m., and said something to the effect that she was going to the market or running an errand. She had run out of the house for some reason, but said she'd be back very shortly.

When I came out of the bathroom and sat down where I had been napping, I looked over at Tammy, and I thought, "I'm not sure she's breathing!" I moved over next to her and felt of her foot. It was cold—her legs were cold from the knees down. I immediately made a telephone call to her doctor, Wallis Marsh, in Pittsburgh, and said, "Wallis, she is gone. She is gone!"

He asked me to go back and check her again. I did that. I went back to the phone and told him. My phone records show that I called Dr. Marsh at, I believe, 7:01 p.m. So it was just minutes after I discovered Tammy that I called him.

I don't recall anything that happened after I discovered her and called the doctor. My housekeeper came back at some point after I talked with my daughter and discovered Tammy, and she [later] said that my little dog and I were just rambling about the house, just in a daze, and all she could hear was me moaning. I was in complete shock. There is so little I remember even about the services.

The Autopsy

Two things that Tammy had always requested of me if she were to predecease me: not to be cremated and not to have an autopsy. After a number of months with all this [controversy] going on, and this was my decision, a very painful one, I decided I would ask the medical examiner to disinter her body and do an autopsy. If you will check public records, you'll see that the medical examiner twice denied the request for an autopsy. Twice. I am the one who faxed the medical examiner, asking him to disinter her body and perform the autopsy. I am the one who did that, who requested it. I didn't have to do that.

It was very painful because she didn't want it. It's totally invasive and it's a horrible thing to witness. Of course, she's in a better place and couldn't care less. But when she was here, she certainly did not want that. It was a terribly painful decision I did make to try to "give the answers" to the girls that they said they were looking for.

The Show Must Go On

Some have said that I forced Tammy back on the stage too soon after her hospitalizations and sicknesses. It was Tammy's doing, of course. She needed that applause—she lived for it. There were many times that I would plead with her to allow me to cancel dates and she would say, "No, I've got to do this. I can't do this to my fans. I cannot do it. I cannot do it."

It was certainly not me saying, "You must do it, you must do it."

Never one time did I ever do that.

Stand By Your Man: Tammy and Hillary Clinton

Tammy was as surprised as I was when Hillary Clinton brought up Tammy's name during a *60 Minutes* TV interview that discussed the accusations Gennifer Flowers had made concerning improper advances by Bill Clinton. "I'm not sitting here, some little woman standing by my man like Tammy Wynette," Hillary Clinton had said.

Tammy took great offense to that comment and how it made her appear. She wanted to know why she was being dragged into this Clinton controversy that she had absolutely nothing to do with. When Hillary Clinton called to apologize, Tammy didn't want to talk to her. I don't blame her.

Finally, Tammy's friend Burt Reynolds intervened on Hillary's behalf and pleaded with Tammy to accept Hillary's call. Tammy did—and she accepted Hillary Clinton's prfound apology.

Tammy and Richey: For the Good Times

On a professional side, I remember the times I would be backstage and see her just slay an audience. And I'd come to the realization all of a sudden, "That's not my wife! That's Tammy Wynette!" I'd be re-impressed and reminded of her enormous talent and magnificent charm that she had. She loved people, she loved fans. She was a gracious person, a very generous, giving soul.

I can remember all the many wonderful vacations that she and I would go on. We had great times on either private ships or cruise ships or going around the world on vacation.

I had a great life with her. I can tell you categorically that Tammy Wynette was always loved by me and adored by me. The only way I ever touched her was with love and gratitude to her for being my companion.

I think I honored Tammy throughout my life with her. I cherished her.

Chapter 10

Naomi Judd's Loving Tribute to Tammy Wynette

Tammy and Naomi:
Soul Sisters of Song and Motherhood

Tammy Wynette's influence on the country music industry extended far beyond millions of fans worldwide who adored her as one of the most distinctive artists in any form of music anywhere. Fellow stars were drawn to her both by her incredible talent and her loving personality. One of those stars is Naomi Judd, whose friendship with Tammy dates back 20 years ago to the very beginning of The Judds' career.

As a family, The Judds rate three stars: the multitalented Naomi, and her daughters, super-singer Wynonna and red-hot Hollywood actress Ashley Judd. The stage glamour, delightful quirkiness and impeccable blood harmonies sent The Judds on a torrid streak with 14 No. 1 records and eight awards from the Country Music Association during their reign at the top. When chronic hepatitis forced Naomi to stop performing in 1991, Wynonna went into what she later described as the "Wynonna Alona" period of her profession. She blossomed as a solo act, hitting No. 1 with her first three records, while wowing audiences and critics alike.

Tammy Wynette put her indelible brand and blessing on both of the singing Judds, starting early in the critical first stages of their show business introduction, when it meant so much to the unknown singers who had recently moved to Nashville from Kentucky via Hollywood. When I asked Naomi for her take on Tammy, she responded with a treasure trove of tales.

Wy and I Meet the First Lady of Country Music

In 1983, Wynonna and I were hanging out at the deejay convention at the Opryland Hotel in Nashville, amusing ourselves since no one was interested in talking to us then. We had just signed with RCA Records, and no one knew or cared who we were.

Suddenly, the room crackled with electricity as the buzz went out that the First Lady of Country Music, Tammy Wynette, had entered.

Wynonna and I had been fascinated by Tammy's voice, the melodrama of her personal life, her wigs, her outlandish country queen costumes—and we couldn't believe our good fortune of suddenly being in the same room. Wynonna had always been intrigued by the height of her hair, the length of the fringe of her outfits, the number of rhinestones.

Tammy's album covers were mini-masterpieces of country camp art. I was always intrigued by the fact that Tammy also had gotten married at age 17, was a struggling single mom when she came to Nashville with her three girls, and was always on the heartbreak highway.

Neither Wy nor I could summon the nerve to approach Tammy, but serendipitously, she turned and we found ourselves face to face. She smiled warmly and said, "Well, hey!"

And thus began our immediate conversation about what it was like to be a singing, traveling mom. I told her Wynonna and I were getting ready to buy our first bus and hit the road, yet I had a bittersweet predicament since I had to leave Ashley at home so she could attend school.

There was a transformation in Tammy's face as she suddenly went from being the country superstar to a mom, relating to another mom. She told me that I would miss birthday parties and proms and that Ashley would get mad at me, that I would call to check on test scores, etc., from truck stops all across America. Yet she said that by being a career mom, we would be able to give our girls a lifestyle that they would never be able to enjoy otherwise.

I told Tammy my dream for Ashley was to be able to put her through college and put braces on her teeth. She smiled as she shared with me what it had been like with her girls. We somehow clicked.

An Award Graced by Tammy's Touch

Later, it was Tammy, along with Ray Stevens, at the 1984 CMA Awards, who presented us with the Horizon Award, our first-ever honor. She told me backstage she hoped she hadn't shown favoritism when she expressed such delight at reading our name on the envelope. If you look back at the videotape, however, you can see the favoritism in her exclamation as she saw our name.

One evening my husband Larry came into the bedroom after I had been on the phone gabbing with a girlfriend for about an hour and a half. He said, "I heard you all share recipes, talk about your problems and delights and motherhood, get tips on good fabric stores, talk about hair products and discuss the status of the country music industry, among other topics." Then he asked, "Who in the world have you been talking to?"

My response, of course, was Tammy.

We enjoyed a privileged conversation. She felt totally safe unloading her stories about her kids in the same way I trusted her discretion in discussing Wy and Ashley.

I remember flashes of irony one time when I was sitting on Tammy's bed playing with her little dog Killer, just hanging out with her. And all of a sudden, I realized this is Tammy Wynette! Suddenly, we would be just your average women, completely in the moment and enjoying each other's company.

Once she called and was telling me that Tina, one of her daughters, had just moved to Nashville from Florida. Tammy said she had taken her grandkids to the Burlington Coat Factory in 100 Oaks Mall to buy them coats to begin the school year since they were not used to the Tennessee winters. All of a sudden she said, "Oh, gosh! I've got to jump off the phone and pack because I hear the bus out front!"

It was that constant ordinary—Tammy, the mom, wife, grandmother image—that contrasted with the country music legend.

Charter Members of the Plank Club

In 1995, George Richey, Tammy's husband, called me one night in a panic. She had been admitted to the Intensive Care Unit at Baptist Hospital in Nashville with a severe infection. When I entered the hospital, although I am a registered nurse who specialized in intensive care, I was badly shaken to see Tammy on life support.

Because of the ventilator, she couldn't speak. I gently took down the right bed rail, pulled up a chair, leaned across and took her hand. I spoke to her about what a wonderful daughter she had been to her mother Mildred. I was privileged to know Tammy's mother, and I let Tammy know how wonderful I thought she had been to bring her mother into her home to care for her around the clock in Mildred's last years.

There were other private thoughts I shared and I will keep private. And I plugged in a nightlight of a guardian angel directly across from Tammy's hospital bed. The warm golden glow cast a soft spell as I told Tammy that it was to remind her of the countless legions of fans who were holding her up in prayer. It was at that moment that big tears streamed down my friend's face.

That night I became aware that Tammy was not destined to live to old age.

She and I rarely talked about our illnesses. Neither of us believed in complaining, and we wanted nothing to do with such negativity. We did, however, agree that we were charter members of the "Plank Club."

It was Tammy who made this observation, saying that she and I had both walked out to the end of the plank and looked down and had seen the dark, murky, shark-filled waters, and then were tapped on the shoulder and summoned back at the last minute. I chided her, gently urging her to live to a ripe old age alongside of me so that we could both be a problem to our kids in our old age.

"Paybacks are hell," Tammy would laugh.

The Liz Taylor of Country Music

Once when she was going through a scary bout with her illnesses, I could tell that the pain and the in-and-out hospitalizations were getting to her. Attempting to make her laugh, I said, "What are you trying to be? The Liz Taylor of country music? Here you are, in and out of hospitals, married multiple times, once to your co-star, you've done the Betty Ford Clinic for your addiction to painkillers because of your illnesses. You've managed to continually transform yourself through fashion stages and remained glamorous for the public and you still have loyal, diehard fans."

Her reaction? Tammy did the bent-over-double belly laugh. She had the most wonderful laugh.

Our "License" to Have Fun

There are so many fond memories of our times together. When Randy Travis, Wynonna, Tammy and I toured together on the GMC Tour, we'd eat crew dinners together and park our buses side by side. If we were tired of, or dreading, putting on pantyhose and makeup on those hot summer nights for state fairs, we had a private signal as time came to jump on the buses and do our makeovers. She'd wink at me as we climbed aboard our individual Silver Eagles and holler, "Well, I've still got my beautician's license."

And I'd call back, "Yep, still got my RN license."

Indeed, it wasn't until the '80s that we both had let our licenses become inactive. However, we still carried them in our billfolds.

Hash Browns or Grits?

Everyone around Tammy and Richey was keenly aware of the utter devotion they had for each other. I recall one Sunday morning as we pulled into Shreveport, Louisiana, and parked at the Holiday Inn. I was just coming out of my bedroom on the bus when Wynonna, who had risen earlier, came on, chortling about something. At the Sunday noon buffet inside the hotel, she had witnessed Richey going through the buffet line, talking into his walkie-talkie.

As Wy got closer to eavesdrop, Richey would speak into his walkie-talkie. "Hash browns or grits?" He'd hold the walkie-talkie up to his ear, put some grits on the plate he was holding and then go on to the next item. "Scrambled eggs or fried?" he would ask.

When Wynonna asked Richey what he was doing, he said that Tammy was still in her nightgown on the bus and he was taking her breakfast to her.

Tammy's Talented Pinky Finger

Sometimes Wy and I would sit on the monitors on the side of the stage and watch Tammy perform. Wynonna would comment, "That woman has more soul in her pinky finger than all of us other chick wannabes combined."

When we would give Tammy her after-show hug and tell her what a great show she had done, Tammy was always characteristically humble. She really acted like an aunt to Wynonna. She was one of those people who you really feel like you've known your whole life—like family.

Biscuits in the Morning...Baby Showers at Night

I want people to know this about Tammy. I want them to know that she made biscuits in the morning. I want them to know that she was always there for her friends.

Last summer she threw a baby shower for Faith Hill at her home. Tammy was not well, yet the place was delightfully decorated and she was the most gracious hostess.

As everyone was leaving that night, Tammy motioned for Ashley and me to come into her bedroom suite for a private visit. I felt very protective of her. I motioned to Ashley that we could only stay a minute because her voice was waning, and it was obvious that she was lacking in energy. I begged her to take care of herself and fussed at her to slow down.

"It's my life," she said plaintively as she hugged me good night in the front doorway. "Country music is my life."

Special Rites for a Special Lady

I was on the road when my husband called me about 10 p.m. on April 6 to let me know that Tammy had crossed over. Nancy Jones, George's wife, had called Wy's house to tell us the devastating news.

I flew home immediately to the private family/close friends funeral service at Judson Baptist Church, a house away from Tammy's home. Wynonna flew in from New York and came straight from the airport to the church. She apologized for wearing pants to the funeral service before she acknowledged Richey, Tammy's girls—Gwen, Jackie, Tina and Georgette—and her stepchildren sitting in the front pew. Dolly Parton and Loretta Lynn were there, too, along with so many of Tammy's friends.

Wynonna's rendition of "How Great Thou Art" elicited cries and audible moans from the family. Dolly was unable to finish her song "Shine On" that she had co-written with Tammy. Loretta told me she was too distraught to sing. Loretta was also upset that Tammy had never been inducted into the Country Music Hall of Fame before she died. For that matter, I added, neither had Dolly at that time.

Lorrie Morgan did a beautiful rendition of "Amazing Grace" and J. D. Sumner and the Stamps Quartet, Jake Hess and the Gaither Vocal Band all contributed beautiful southern gospel numbers. Since George Richey comes out of southern gospel, it was appropriate that the Oak Ridge Boys and these other established gospel groups be part of her funeral service.

After the moving message and song tributes, Crystal Gayle, Bill Anderson, Jan Howard, Garth Brooks, Trisha Yearwood, Gary Chapman, Loretta, Dolly, Randy Travis, Ralph Emery and others stood in the church, hugging one another and telling each other that we loved each other.

It was a moment I will never forget.

One Final Gift—Friends

After the public memorial service at the Ryman Auditorium in downtown Nashville, I dropped off food at Tammy's house—cornbread, chicken and rice, salads, a cake and a pie and a couple of vegetable casserole dishes. When I returned home late Thursday night, just as I was taking off my funeral clothes, the phone rang.

"Hello, my name is Johnny Cash," the voice on the other end said.

Johnny was having a low-energy day and had been unable to come to the services. He just wanted to talk to somebody. My friend and I spoke for about 45 minutes, and as we hung up, we told each other that we loved each other.

Loretta invited me to come and visit her in Hurricane Mills. I cancelled some other plans so I could go.

Tammy's premature passing has made me even more keenly aware of how important friends are.

America is losing its sense of community.

But the country music family, thank God, is not losing that vital gift. Tammy, in death as in life, made that sense of community even stronger for all of us.

I miss my fellow charter member of the Plank Club that she created for us. I miss her laughter, I miss her music, I miss her friendship, and I miss her love.

As she told Ashley and me during that private visit, "Country music is my life."

And country music is so much richer for the good fortune and honor of having been blessed with Tammy Wynette as its First Lady.

Goodbye, my friend.

Chapter 11

Charlie Monk:
The Mayor of Music Row

Country Music's Favorite Character

George Strait, Vince Gill, Reba McEntire, Alabama, the Dixie Chicks, Travis Tritt, Brooks & Dunn, Keith Whitley, Brad Paisley, Chely Wright, Tracy Byrd, Lorrie Morgan, LeAnn Rimes, Patty Loveless, Dwight Yoakam, Faith Hill, Toby Keith, Tim McGraw, Jo Dee Messina, Martina McBride...the list runs on.

An All-Star lineup, for sure, and all rose to fame with the help of performances on the Country Radio Seminar's New Faces Show emceed by Charlie Monk. His first-name friendship with country's hottest stars and top executives earned him the honorary title of "Mayor of Music Row." Monk's offbeat personality, outspoken honesty, affable nature and quick wit endear him to those who inhabit the Nashville music world.

*The "Mayor of Music Row." Charlie Monk, left, greets some of his
loyal followers, Brad Paisley, Garth Brooks and Eddy Arnold.
(Photo courtesy of Gerry Wood)*

A former country music deejay, Monk has a background
in music licensing and publishing. He now owns his own
company, Monk Family Music. Through the years he signed
up such talents as Randy Travis, Aaron Tippin and Kenny
Chesney when they were just kids with a dream, stalking
the streets of Nashville trying to get someone to listen to
their songs.

"I'm the luckiest guy in Nashville because I've made a
living doing what I enjoy," Monk told me. "Honestly, I'm a
show business groupie who loves hanging around talented
people and feeding off all their creative energy."

Monk Has Friends in New Faces

Monk's often biting humor shines during the annual New Faces Show, a launching pad for usually unknown artists who sometimes later shape the destiny of country music. Many of them graduate from Who's That? to Who's Who in Country Music with commanding performances in front of the important, but hard to please, audience of radio executives and deejays. Their few moments on stage will have a tremendous impact on how much radio airplay their records receive.

Riveting performances paid off quickly for some acts, including Alabama, struggling on a small independent label in 1975. The group quickly landed a major deal with RCA Records and soon became one of country music's most successful acts.

"The biggest impact," observed Monk, "was Randy Travis in 1986, because he changed the way the whole Nashville community regarded the back-to-the-basics traditional side of country music. Another standout was Tim McGraw in 1994."

The show's history dates back to 1970, but no future star emerged until Crystal Gayle broke through the next year. Charlie Monk now takes us back to some of the greatest talent-rich years of the New Faces Show:

"After Eddie Rabbit appeared in 1975, he soon landed his first No. 1 hit. When Alabama, Juice Newton, Sylvia and Reba McEntire performed in 1980, nobody knew anything about them. They all went on to careers that won top awards, along with gold and platinum album sales. George Strait was the hit of the 1982 show, and that resulted, three months later, in his first No. 1 record, 'Fool Hearted Memory.'

Vince Gill
(© MCA Nashville)

"I thought Vince Gill was kind of lackluster when he did the show in 1985, but before the year was over, he scored with his first two Top Ten singles. Two years later, Dwight Yoakam, who was the bad boy of country music back then, rehearsed two songs—the limit for the acts to sing. Then he went onstage and sang *eight* songs. I thought we were going to have to get the hook to get him offstage. The next year was just great with four out of the ten acts later landing records on the top of the charts—Patty Loveless, K.T. Oslin, Ricky Van Shelton and Schuyler, Knobloch and Bickhardt.

"The year of 1990 was also talent-laden with Travis Tritt, Mary Chapin Carpenter, Lorrie Morgan and Suzy Bogguss. But the biggest year for breakout artists was 1992. Six of the acts later went No. 1—Collin Raye, Pam Tillis, Tracy Lawrence, Little Texas, Sammy Kershaw and Brooks and Dunn. They sang 'Boot Scootin' Boogie' which I didn't think would do anything for them. Guess I was wrong, huh?

"One of the bravest performances came in 1994 when John Berry refused to let severe headaches stop him from singing 'Your Love Amazes Me.' His a capella version of the song received a thunderous standing ovation. Just days later, John was rushed to the hospital for brain surgery. The 1997 talent parade showcased Jo Dee Messina, David Kersh, Deana Carter, Kevin Sharp, Trace Adkins and young newcomer LeAnn Rimes, who sang 'Blue.'

"Next year the hit act was the Dixie Chicks, whose career rocketed following the show. They rose all the way to the top, but they might not stay there because of Natalie Maines's comments about President Bush during the Iraq war. That really backfired on them, at least in the country market.

Trick Pony
(© Warner Bros. Records Inc.)

"In more recent years those making points with the radio rulers have been Brad Paisley, Chris Cagle, Trick Pony, Sara Evans, Montgomery Gentry, Keith Urban, SHeDAISY and Allison Moorer.

"It has been an incredible experience to witness the early victories in the careers of these artists, and it has been sad to see that the majority of those appearing on the show never made it to the big leagues of country music. There's only so much room on the radio play lists, the charts and the record store bins, so some will just have to return to their home towns and their day gigs. But the New Faces Show has been, and always will be, the top venue for anyone with the talent, drive and determination to make it all the way to the top, and the desire to get there fast."

The Mayor of Mirth Minces the Mighty

Between acts on the New Faces Show, emcee Charlie Monk takes the microphone to lance and deflate the sometimes-fragile egos of stars and executives alike. Spotting legendary producer Jimmy Bowen, Monk quipped, "Jimmy Bowen is to country music what Saddam Hussein was to world peace." He aimed arrows at broadcasting great Ralph Emery by claiming, "The difference between Elvis Presley and Ralph Emery is that there's a good possibility that Elvis is still alive."

In prime form at the 2003 show, Monk scored laughter with these zingers:

• "In honor of ZZ Top going country, let's mention some other people who have tried to go country this year—Kid Rock, Sheryl Crow…and *Faith Hill.*"

• "Dick Clark shot himself in the foot with the Osbourne Family hosting the American Music Awards. He said he would not make the same mistake with the Academy of Country Music Awards. The host will be Anna Nicole Smith."

• "The Tim McGraw and Elton John duet was the best moment of the Grammy Awards telecast. But, I'm wondering, are we supposed to address Elton as *Sir* Elton or *Lady* Elton?"

•"Did you know that Trace Adkins, Terri Clark and Deana Carter graduated Summa Cum Laude from their DUI class?"

•"The last time I saw Shania Twain she asked me, 'Charlie, if you had three wishes, what would your other two be?'

Mayor Monk on the Move at Fan Fair

Charlie Monk's rapid-fire one-liners accompany him wherever he travels, including his visits to the International Country Music Fan Fair staged each year in Nashville. During one of these fan fests I followed Hizzoner and captured some of his banter.

Stopping by the Oak Ridge Boys' fan booth, Monk asked Oak Ridge Boy Duane Allen, "How can you call four 40-year-old guys 'boys'?" Charlie left while Duane was deeply pondering the question and its ramifications on the group's name.

The Mayor kissed Pam Tillis as fans crowded around her booth for autographs, chats and photos. Referring to Pam's father, Mel Tillis, Monk yelled out to her faithful followers, "I dated Pam's father in high school." Laughing, Pam shoved Charlie away. The quipster headed for the Bryan White location, where he informed the fan club staffers, "I actually have socks that are older than Bryan White."

Monk then ran into Kenny Chesney, an artist he helped guide toward a record label contract. "What's the most amazing thing you've learned from me about your music career?" he asked. Kenny thought for a second, and then answered, "What I learned from you is not reportable." Chesney chuckled and quickly added, "Actually, you told me, 'Don't be serious.' And that really helps me from time to time."

Pam Tillis
(© Sony Music Entertainment Inc.)

Fascinated by Martina McBride's exhibit set up like a 1950s-era kitchen, Charlie opened the refrigerator door and took a whiff of the musky odor. "Whoa!" he complained to McBride, "This refrigerator smells like my mother-in-law."

Victoria Shaw's display served as the last stop for the Mayor of Music Row. "I've performed at three Fan Fairs and snuck into ten," the vivacious redheaded singer-songwriter confessed to the only Monk in the building. "I would sneak backstage and figure some way to slip in." Charlie turned to the fans waiting in line for their favorite singer, and informed them, "Victoria has a great twist on her music career. She's a Los Angeles gal who moved to New York to work as a saloon singer, and later came to Nashville to be a star and then became a songwriter."

"Nobody wanted me back then," Victoria explained, a cloud of hurt chasing her smile away. And then she directed an unexpected compliment to someone who had helped her when she was an unknown talent looking for a break. "But Charlie, way in the beginning, you were one of the first people to show me any kindness and encouragement. You let me use your office to make demo tapes, use the phone, get paper clips and anything else I needed. And you introduced me around to other people who helped me, too."

The King of Zingers, the Mayor of Music Row demonstrated that he is an equal opportunity jokester by targeting himself. "She's been a hell of a lot more successful since she left my office," Charlie Monk told the Victoria Shaw fans.

Victoria's face beamed and blushed.

Then her expression turned to surprise as Monk handed her a beautiful bouquet of flowers. He received a kiss and a hug.

Monk is one Mayor who is a shoo-in for re-election.

Chapter 12

Ashes to Ashes,
Bluegrass to Bluegrass

Bill Monroe's Last Curtain Call

Country music stars can stage one hell of a funeral. I've had the sad privilege of attending several, including the services for Tammy Wynette, Chet Atkins and Bill Monroe, who died on September 9, 1996. Tammy's was gut-grabbing emotional as her distraught husband George Richey reeled with grief. Chet Atkins would have loved his own ceremonies, made memorable by the touching tribute from his friend Garrison Keillor of *Prairie Home Companion* fame. And Bill Monroe was dispatched up yonder by a rollicking musical sendoff from his friends and fellow performers.

Held at the historic Ryman Auditorium where the Father of Bluegrass Music picked and played on the Grand Ole Opry stage from the 1930s until the show gravitated to

Opryland in 1974, the service was simple and simply stunning. More than a thousand greats, family and fans paid homage to the Country Music Hall of Fame member, a genius who invented a music style that thrives to this day.

The time-worn Ryman pews comforted a galaxy of stars, including Grandpa Jones, Earl Scruggs, Skeeter Davis, Little Jimmy Dickens and Steve Earle.

Monroe's powder blue casket was closed for the service and topped with his white cowboy hat. A forest of flowers and Monroe's mandolin sat silent and serene alongside the coffin at the foot of the stage. The mourners read the printed program that quoted appropriate lyrics from an old Monroe song: "I'm going back to old Kentucky where the skies are always blue..."

Blue skies and bluegrass bracketed a lot of blue people fighting back tears as the service progressed. But moods changed as the expected tributes—"Since Bill Monroe died, there's a lot more bluegrass playing in heaven"—gave way to the magical healing power of music. Vince Gill, Ricky Skaggs, Marty Stuart, Stuart Duncan and Roy Huskey, Jr. took the stage for a powerful version of "Working on a Building." Vince stayed on stage as Emmylou Harris joined him for a commanding rendition of "Wayfaring Stranger." Another bluegrass legend, Ralph Stanley, sang "Rank Stranger," followed by the heaven-sent voice of Alison Krauss with "A Beautiful Life."

The tear-jerking highlight came with Connie Smith's heart-tugging version of "How Great Thou Art," breathtaking as it echoed off the hallowed walls and rafters of the historic Ryman. Vince Gill teamed with Ricky Skaggs and Patty Loveless for the meaningful "Go Rest High on that Mountain."

Friends related humorous and significant stories about Monroe, and the mood slowly began to swing from sad toward celebration.

"If this seems inappropriate, we're sorry," Skaggs said, igniting a raucous rendition of Monroe's "Rawhide." Hands were clapping, feet were tapping and spirits soaring as Skaggs, Gill and Marty Stuart brought the mourners to their feet in applause. Even in death, Bill Monroe had stirred his last Ryman audience into a standing ovation.

Three bagpipe players marched down the aisle toward the casket, playing the haunting "Amazing Grace." Then the Ryman grew deathly silent as the casket was wheeled slowly up the aisle to an open door. As it passed out the door, Bill Monroe's eternal musical spirit went with it. You could almost hear a faint and ghostly "woooshhh" as the auditorium, despite the large crowd, suddenly seemed empty and void of sound, a musical vacuum.

The next day, only hours before what would have been his 85th birthday, the Father of Bluegrass was buried in the rich soil of his hometown of Rosine, Kentucky—six feet deep, beneath the grass of his beloved Bluegrass State.

Fire in His Bones

A day after the burial, I talked to Ricky Skaggs as he fought through sorrow over the death of his mentor, Bill Monroe. Ricky had been with Monroe during his final hours of life. Sometimes with his voice cracking, other times growing cheerful with happy memories and the knowledge that a unique master had been his teacher, Ricky revealed to me an incredible tale about his relationship with Bill Monroe. Here it is, in his own words.

The last few times I saw Mr. Monroe he still had fire in his bones. There were times I was there to see him that he would play the mandolin and he was trying to write. So there was life, excitement and creativity still left in the marrow of his bones like the patriarchs of old.

The last time I saw him was three days before he died. I handed him the mandolin. He did not want to play it. I knew then that he really wanted to go home. If he didn't want to play, he was ready to go.

I made him a promise that day. I told him not to worry about the music, because it's in great shape. I promised him as long as I live I'm going to play bluegrass music. I know one of us will always play it. There's no way you can kill it.

I said, "Bill, I'm going to tell people about you everywhere I go—not that I haven't already. I'm going to make sure people hear the name Bill Monroe and always tell them that you started this music. So don't worry about it."

There was certainly an air of respect and honor at the Ryman funeral. He wouldn't have loved just a real straight somber thing. He had total respect, but he also felt so strong that his music was a gift that it didn't matter what kind of tune it was—it was still as precious as a gospel song. He really respected so much the gift that was there. He knew where it came from. He was a special man that way.

Standing on the stage looking down at his casket, I felt like he was watching us. Bill would have wanted people to remember him in happy times as well. He was a man who commanded so much respect. He didn't command you to respect him—it was just something that naturally came along with him.

I lost it when we kicked into "Rawhide." It came out of the depths of my guts. All these years I had wondered what it was about bluegrass music that really drew me to it, made me love it, made me want to follow it and play it the rest of my life. All the questions were answered right there. Because I suddenly realized it wasn't the songs, it wasn't the singing—it was that aggressive, fiery excitement and vigor in the playing and picking.

That's what drew me to the mandolin. The instrumental thing had turned me on and made me fall in love with his music. As small as it was, what a seed planter that mandolin became.

When those bagpipes started playing and they began hauling him out, I sensed such an honor of God. It was like, "You think *this* is something, you should have been here when we ushered him *in* the Ryman!" It was like a patriarch. A president. A general. There was a royalty that left country music. His spirit touched us all.

Bill Monroe was my teacher. The last time he and I had lunch together was in eastern Kentucky where I have a project going to provide food, clothing and education for Appalachian families. We walked into this little place and he introduced me to everybody. He said, "Y'all know this man right here, Ricky Skaggs? He's from Kentucky and he's powerful."

We sat down and ordered our lunch. He asked me, "You got change for two dollars?" I told him I didn't, so he went to the cash register and asked for two dollars in quarters. He then went from table to table, and wherever there was a little kid, he would give these children quarters.

A guy came up to me and said, "Hey, Ricky, how are you doing today?"

I told him, "Well, I'm just sitting, watching the teacher. I'm his student again. He's teaching me how to be. And how to be humble."

I've cried some this week. I was eating breakfast listening to the radio and heard "Wayfaring Stranger." Just hearing Bill sing this song that was probably cut back in the mid-50s got to me. He always sang about going home, that place far away where my mother is, where my father is, where my Lord is. Now he's really there. Man, I lost it again and just started crying.

I got up and put my dishes in the sink and I looked outside. A red Kentucky cardinal was sitting in this tree right by the porch. Just looking in the window at me. I thought, "That's it! He's just letting me know that it's okay. That whenever I come, he's going to be there waiting for me." I had myself a good cry.

I'm keeping the promise I made to Bill. Any time we do bluegrass on the road, we're always going to do Bill Monroe, the Stanley Brothers and Flatt and Scruggs songs.

And any time I see a Kentucky cardinal, I'll certainly think of him.

He was that red bird that was easily noticed.

Chapter 13

Country Comedy Cuts to the Chase

A Lasting Legacy of Laughter

Country folks have enjoyed, and created, comedy for centuries, dating back to the storytelling days of Appalachian pioneers and latter day tale spinners such as Mark Twain and Will Rogers, who combined wit and wisdom to move beyond laughter into logic.

That tradition has continued through the years in all forms of entertainment incarnations—from Vaudeville to the Grand Ole Opry, from western movie sidekicks like Andy Devine and Gabby Hayes, from the *Beverly Hillbillies* to *Hee Haw*, from Andy Griffith to Jerry Clower, from Stringbean to Grandpa Jones, from Judy Canova to Minnie Pearl, from Jeff Foxworthy to Bill Engvall, from Ray Stevens to Cledus T. Judd, from Don Bowman to Lewis Grizzard, and from Homer and Jethro to Pinkard and Bowden.

Mark Twain would fit right in these days as a philosopher in residence. Give him a topic, and he would have a quick take on it:

Cledus T. Judd
(© Sony Music Entertainment Inc.)

Dogs: "If you pick up a starving dog and make him prosperous, he will not bite you. This is the principal difference between a dog and a man."

Dogs, Part Two: "Heaven goes by favor. If it went by merit, you would stay out and your dog would go in."

Behavior: "Be good and you will be lonesome."

Temptation: "It is easier to stay out than get out."

Kindness and Drinking: "Never refuse to do a kindness unless the act would work great injury to yourself, and never refuse to take a drink—under any circumstances."

Will Rogers could find modern day relevance with such political potshots as: "I belong to no organized party. I am a Democrat."

Minnie Pearl used this one for decades: "He paid me a compliment. He said I looked like a breath of spring. Well, he didn't use them words. He said I looked like the end of a hard winter."

Famed for his "You're a redneck if…" routines, Jeff Foxworthy has proclaimed that he's not a jealous type of guy: "I have never been jealous. Not even when my dad finished fifth grade a year before I did!"

Pinkard and Bowden took country hits and mangled them into hilarious oblivion. When Willie Nelson revived the old classic, "Blue Eyes Crying in the Rain," Sandy Pinkard and Richard Bowden couldn't wait to anoint the evergreen classic with their special treatment, creating a road rage saga about little old ladies driving down the interstate:

"In the taillights' glow I see 'em,
Blue hairs driving in my lane
When she hit me and departed
I knew there'd be no insurance claim."

Gerry Wood, Jerry Clower and Clower's manager Tandy
Rice at a book-signing event for Ain't God Good!
(Photo courtesy of Gerry Wood)

High on Clower Power

Writing two books with country comedian Jerry
Clower—*Ain't God Good!* and *Let The Hammer Down!*—
provided me with a profound admiration for the man and
his humor. I've seen people high on booze. I've seen them
high on drugs. But Clower's natural high—a near-constant
energy peak—was a high that came from on high.

He didn't drink, smoke, pop pills, toke joints, cuss or
chase women. Sound dull? Don't believe it.

Charged by religion, fired by enthusiasm and guided by his coveted Good Book, Clower roared on like a one-man SWAT squad for laughter, love and the Lord.

Jerry backed into show business by enhancing his sales pitch for Mississippi Chemical's fertilizer by telling high-octane anecdotes fueled by his Southern heritage. Clower's MCA Records albums sold millions; he frequently visited the top network and syndicated television and radio shows; and his commercials sold tons of dog food and trucks. A popular member of the Grand Ole Opry cast, Jerry claimed Nashville as his second home, but never moved away from his Mississippi heartland.

Jerry Clower was a huge man, a huge presence. He could walk alone into the Super Bowl and fill it up with his size, personality and high-decibel whooping and hollering. And when it came to telling stories—many with a moral hidden slyly amidst the laughter—no one surpassed "The Mouth of the South."

The man who turned fertilizer peddling into fertile platinum albums died in 1998 at the age of 71. Spending days with Jerry as he showed me the sites and sights of his rural Mississippi childhood adventures, I knew him well enough to realize that he would want to leave his fans laughing. For that reason, I'll relate these Jerry Clower yarns that he told me and relayed to the world through his albums, books, broadcast appearances and concerts. As a tribute to Jerry and his love of provoking laughter, here are some of my favorites.

Plumbing for Profit

A doctor friend of mine told me that he needed a plumber mighty bad. He called for a plumber and finally got one after three weeks.

The plumber came during the Christmas holidays and unclogged all of the pipes in ten minutes. The water was running and everything was fine.

"Mr. Plumber, don't send me a bill," the doctor said. "Tell me, how much do I owe you?"

"Seventy-five dollars."

"Seventy-five dollars? Why you haven't worked ten minutes! I'm a doctor and I don't make that kind of money."

"When I was a doctor, *I* didn't make that kind of money either," answered the plumber.

Big Bucks in Cockleburrs

Some of my favorite stories are about people who think they're fooling somebody else only to discover that the shoe is on the other foot.

One year New-Gene Ledbetter went off on a big 4-H Club Roundup up in Chicago. He told his papa, Uncle Virsi, that he had to take things to swap with some of the other boys coming in from states all over the country.

Some of those Yankee 4-H Club boys were making fun of those Southern farm boys. But when New-Gene came back, he had $387, all in one-dollar bills.

Uncle Virsi got a dried brush broom. "New-Gene, you done robbed the bank."

"I ain't no such, Poppa. I ain't done nothing wrong. I just took advantage of some ignorant people. I can't help it if they're crazy."

"Well, how did you get this money?"

"Daddy, I took a big sack of cockleburs with me. I sold them to them Yankee boys for a dollar apiece as porcupine eggs."

How Now Brown Cow?

A big record executive at MCA in Hollywood said, "Jerry, I sure would love to go bird hunting."

I told him the best quail hunting in the whole world is in southwest Mississippi. So he flew to Jackson, and when he got off the jet, he had his hunting clothes on. He looked like Little Lord Fauntleroy.

We got in the car and went down to Route 4, Liberty, to the beautiful Virsi Ledbetter farm. I drove up into his yard. "Excuse me just a minute, sir, let me tell Uncle Virsi we're going to be hunting on his place."

I went in and Uncle Virsi was so glad to see me. "Welcome, son. I hope you kill a bunch of them."

"Thank you, Uncle Virsi."

I started out the door and Uncle Virsi started crying. "I'm gonna have to ask you to do something for me, son. Ol' Della, my mule, I made thirty good crops with her. The veterinarian was out here yesterday and said she's dying, and she's suffering. Jerry, would you shoot her for me?"

"Yeah, Uncle Virsi. I don't like to do it, but if she's suffering, I'll shoot her for you."

"You go ahead and shoot her and go on bird hunting, and me and the boys will tend to her late this evening."

On the way back to the car I thought I would have me some fun out of this Hollywood dude.

I got in the car and said, "You know, that old scoundrel told me I couldn't hunt on his place! As good as I've been to him, he's told me, 'No—get you and that Hollywood city slicker away from here.'"

I beat the dashboard with my fists and I scratched off and threw rocks all up the side of his house, got on down the road about a hundred yards and there was old Della grazing. I slammed on the brakes. "Uh-huh, I'll show that old rascal!"

I grabbed my shotgun and jumped out.

BOOM! BOOM!

And down old Della went, graveyard dead.

Just as I turned around and looked over to see what the dude thought, I heard three shots over there.

BOOM! BOOM! BOOM!

"What are you doing?" I yelled.

"That old fellow upset you so bad, Jerry, I killed three of his cows."

Marcel's Hare-Brained Idea

Marcel Ledbetter told me that he has found a cure for baldness.

"I've done figured me out a way to put hair up on top of their head."

"Marcel, how do you do that?" I asked him.

"Well, I get me a quart of alum juice and a quart of green persimmon juice. I mix it together half and half. They'll massage the top of their head with that concoction."

"And it will grow hair on their head?"

"No, but it'll draw their sideburns up on top of their head."

Uncle Looney Better Stay Put

Me and Marcel had to go to the funeral when his Uncle Looney Douglas died. We were sitting by his wife, Aunt Penny. Uncle Looney was up there in the casket.

As the preacher got up to start the service, Aunt Penny started squalling. "Looney, speak to me! Looney, please, raise up, darling. Say something to me!"

Marcel said, "Aunt Penny, if he does, *that* window's mine."

A Fond Farewell to Jerry Clower from Gerry Wood

Jerry Clower opened his heart and his hearth to me during my trips to visit him and his family in Mississippi.

He took me down dusty roads to show me the "baptizing hole" in a creek close to the East Fork Baptist Church. That's where he and the one and only woman in his life, Homerline, were baptized. He introduced me to his friends and neighbors, including Chief Carey Hill who lived next door. Chief Hill was an artist at his trade—welding. I asked him if it were possible to weld a crack in my Franklin fireplace. Chief Hill responded, "I can weld everything except a broken heart and the break of day."

We traveled through the hamlets and hidden byways of old Mississippi, its earth-blood soil and massive greenery reminding me of my old Kentucky home. Through Jerry's wide eyes and unbridled humor, the soul of the Southland revealed itself to me as never before—a lovely land of tragedy, compassion and contradiction that we both loved so much.

And the meals! Take me back! We stopped for lunch at Jerry's mother's house, and the bowls of wonderful home-cooked food stopped by my plate for refills about every 30 seconds. I ate everything that passed by until I looked, and felt, like a Southern-fried Willie Wonka.

I demolished homemade cornpone, biscuits, butter, preserves, molasses, sweet potatoes, rice, onions, turnips covered with hot pepper sauce, chicken and dumplings, lima beans, peaches topped with whipped cream and syrup, fruitcake, pound cake, iced tea and coffee. By the time we finished all that lunch, it was almost time for supper.

Just before Jerry drove me back to the train station in McComb, his beautiful daughter Katy, just a handful of years old then, worried about me getting hungry again on a train bound for Tennessee. She slipped me some of her candy, so I wouldn't starve. I didn't have the heart to tell the sweet child that there was a dining car on board.

At the McComb station, we heard the whistle of the approaching Amtrak passenger train, the New Orleans to Chicago *Panama Limited* that's still running—now under the equally famous name, *City of New Orleans*. With little-boy zeal, Jerry checked his watch and yelled, "On time!" As the streamliner squealed to a stop, Jerry looked wistfully at the gleaming, hissing coach, lounge, diner and Pullman cars and declared, "I wish I could catch the train with you and go all the way to Chicago. We'd get us a room on there and go to the diner. You've got to try the roast beef dinner. You'll love it. Come back and visit any time you want to."

"Okay, Jerry. Tell Katy her candy made an excellent meal for me."

We hugged, shook hands and I hopped aboard.

The *Panama Limited* left so fast that I recalled with a laugh Jerry's tale about how Marcel Ledbetter once boarded this same train in McComb, bound for New Orleans. He stopped on the bottom step, turned around to kiss his mama goodbye, and kissed a bull on the mouth at Hammond, Louisiana.

Clower stories. They never stop.

Even now.

The next time I ride Amtrak from Memphis to New Orleans and we pass through Yazoo City and McComb, I'll see the sights that Jerry shared with me, so proud of his native South. I'll be sad about his passing on, but as the train slides smoothly southbound down the tracks, the sadness will soon depart when I remember his serious and humorous sides.

Jerry Clower will be laughing, too, when he sees me looking for the bull in Hammond.

When we were writing *Ain't God Good!*, Jerry told me, "Everybody ought to be a laughing Christian. I'm convinced that there's just one place where there's not any laughter, and I've made arrangements to miss hell. So ha-ha-ha! And hallelujah! I ain't never going to have to be nowhere where some folks ain't laughing. If you're walking around with a hump in your back and your lips pooched out and you don't believe in laughing, then you ought to go home and look in the mirror and see what all of us other folks been laughing *at* for all these many years."

The Mouth of the South is silent now, but Jerry Clower's laughter is ever after.

Chapter 14

Country Music Math:
Lyrics + Melodies = Money

How Songs are Born

It All Begins With A Song, the motto of the Nashville Songwriters Association International, forms the bedrock of country music. Nowhere is this deceptively simple truism more evident than in Nashville, Tennessee—Music City, USA.

The songwriting profession fuels the country music industry, its stars, recording and management executives, producers, studio engineers, concert promoters, radio programmers...every aspect of this fascinating, and frequently lucrative, business.

Not since the glory days of New York City's Tin Pan Alley have the originators of lyrics and melodies meant so much to the musical life and times of a city and the world outside. These song-slingers, creative guns firing on-target bullets along with errant blanks, embody the lifeblood, heartbeat and soul of country music. Many are, want to be, or will become, artists themselves. That's how Willie Nelson, Tom T. Hall, Victoria Shaw, Phil Vassar, Kix Brooks, Ronnie Dunn, and many others forwarded their careers.

Where do the songs come from? They don't arrive on silver platters ready to be served up to top acts. This is more of a sausage-making, rather than a star-making, enterprise. The process is not so pretty to watch sometimes, but it's the final product that counts.

Some tunes emerge from song factory sessions behind publishing company closed doors, compatible writers placed together—some strong on lyrics, some experts with melodies—who have been tipped off that Trisha Yearwood or George Strait or Tim McGraw needs a slow ballad. Or that Rascal Flatts, Kenny Chesney or Terri Clark seeks a rousing up-tempo number with an attitude.

Successful stars often call their own shots when searching for new material, firm in their belief that they know, better than anyone else, exactly what's needed for the next album or single. Sifting through hundreds of songs, they could err and record a career-damaging stiff, or they might pick the next hit to top the charts.

Then there's the writer burning with a brilliant new idea, a unique coupling of lyrics and a catchy melody, that will snag the attention of the first producer or artist who listens to the demo tape.

Gifted singers with a strong writing talent often take matters into their own hands and pen most of their own songs. That time-proven tradition worked for Hank Williams along with modern-day wordsmiths Garth Brooks and Brad Paisley. At the other end of the spectrum, George Strait in his entire gilded show business career, has recorded only one of his own songs. Dean Dillon and a bevy of writers who have made a small fortune with Strait smashes thank their lucky stars for George's wisdom in song selection.

This is big business, and competitive as hell. A number-one country smash can easily earn its writer—sometimes worried about making that next rent and utility payment—one-quarter of a million dollars.

Because of country music's emphasis on the song, Nashville has become Nirvana for those who write music for a living. They come to Music City from one-horse country towns, cosmopolitan cities like Los Angeles, Dallas and New York, from every state in the country, and from Canada and Europe.

They play their new compositions to friends, family, relatives, and at the plethora of songwriter showcases and writers' nights, ranging from little known dives in Austin to famed listening rooms such as Nashville's Bluebird Café and Douglas Corner. All it takes is one compelling number played at one of these locales to prod a producer, publisher or artist to latch onto it and help launch a new hit into orbit.

Glittering galas that reward the genre's top writers and publishers rival, in attendance and importance, the popular televised Country Music Awards show in Nashville and the Academy of Country Music Awards in Los Angeles and Las Vegas. Appreciative of the hits these writers have created, superstars such as Shania Twain and Tim McGraw rub elbows with the award-winning lyric-driven luminaries at black-tie banquets hosted by Broadcast Music, Inc. (BMI), the American Society of Composers, Authors and Publishers (ASCAP) and the Society of European Stage Authors and Composers (SESAC). These organizations gather performance fees from radio, TV, clubs and other sources and distribute them to their writer and publisher members. Competing for top talent, all three have boosted the emphasis on their Nashville and Southern operations over the past years as the songwriting and publishing epicenter continues to shift from both coasts inward to Nashville.

Vince Gill will sit next to Kris Kristofferson at a BMI Awards banquet. Reba McEntire and Faith Hill will journey to an ASCAP Number One party to honor the creators of Faith's chart-topping smash, published by Reba's company.

Writing on the Run

For all the songs created in the sterile environment of a publishing company office, mini-studio, or the imposing solitude of a writer's own home, there are always happenstance wonders that stretch the borders of the creative birthplace.

Inspired, literally, on the fly, Tom T. Hall grabbed an airplane sickness bag to jot down the lyrics to a song that had just set off a brain-wave light bulb. Thus, the start of his melancholy piece of philosophy, "Old Dogs, Children and Watermelon Wine."

Billy Edd Wheeler, on the road, used a piece of cardboard intended to keep a shirt wrinkle-free, to scribble the lyrics for "Jackson," recorded by Johnny and June Carter Cash.

A pencil and a yellow legal pad captured Jerry Jeff Walker's classic "Mr. Bojangles," including a scratched-out verse.

Kris Kristofferson jotted down "Help Me Make It Through The Night" on a small piece of paper that bore the original lyrics and title of "Help Me Make It Through *To-night*."

Railroaded by Jimmy Buffett and Jerry Jeff Walker

Lefty Frizzell hit the charts with "Railroad Lady," the sad chronology of a train-loving woman on the skids, later released by Merle Haggard, Willie Nelson and its co-authors Jerry Jeff Walker and Jimmy Buffett. Here's the tall, but true, tale of the conception of that song.

The day before the Louisville & Nashville Railroad's passenger train, the *Pan American*, was to depart from New Orleans to Cincinnati, with Nashville as an intermediate stop, I introduced two of my friends to each other: Jimmy Buffett, a struggling songwriter-singer who, in 1970, was having little success convincing Nashville's music moguls to listen to his offbeat, quirky ditties that didn't fit the country mold; and Jerry Jeff Walker, the New York-turned-Key West-turned-Texas troubadour who was in the enviable position of watching his "Mr. Bojangles" dance onto the pop charts, thanks to the Nitty Gritty Dirt Band's powerful version. Walker would become one of the reigning monarchs of Texas music as the Cosmic Cowboy era exploded, and he rules the Lone Star state to this day. Both have enjoyed major country and pop success and have carved out their unique personal musical niches.

Walker knew little about the new friend that he welcomed into his creative community after he met Buffett at what was supposed to be a show at Southern Mississippi University, Jimmy's alma mater. After introducing the talented twosome, I learned what happens when nobody shows

*Jimmy Buffett, left, and Gerry Wood celebrate
at the Master's Golf Tournament in Georgia.
(Photo courtesy of Gerry Wood)*

up for a show—the case on this particular afternoon in Hattiesburg, Mississippi. Two performers and no audience except me, so they uncased their guitars, sat on the edge of the stage and sang songs to each other for a half hour. The unknown Buffett was thrilled to meet a songwriter-singer with the reputation of Walker and ecstatic when his songs gained praise from a seasoned veteran. I played the role of an audience of one.

Following the "show," we ventured into New Orleans for a night on the town. On Bourbon Street we ran into Toad Andrews of Tracy Nelson's band, Mother Earth. What a coincidence! I was his Nashville landlord. Toad was lord of the guitar, often picking bluesy chords with his teeth, biting and sliding along the strings of the instrument. He presented quite a sight as he lifted the instrument to his face and went to work, chomping away.

Toad, Jerry Jeff, Jimmy and I prowled the wilderness of Bourbon Street on a full-moon night, and anyone who has had the experience of exploring a pregnant-mooned Crescent City knows the dangers inherent in that combustible combination. We added our own lunar-howling personas to the witches brew.

At 3:13 a.m. in a small bar, a folk singer onstage paused to announce, "Well, Jerry Jeff Walker once dropped by one of my shows and taught me how to sing this song—'Mr. Bojangles.'"

I nudged Jerry Jeff standing next to me at the bar, as we downed various versions of rum drinks, fast and hard, except for Walker who drank Wild Turkey on the rocks, slow and steady. "Jerry Jeff, when did that happen?"

Walker looked up from his drink, squinted at the entertainer who rendered a so-so rendition of Bojangles, and advised, "It didn't happen. I've never seen that guy before in my life, much less taught him how to sing Bojangles."

As Jerry Jeff's eyes focused intensely on the entertainer, I knew he was going to pursue the matter further. The show ended after two more rounds of drinks, and Jerry Jeff walked to the stage and stuck out his hand. The singer looked at him with no sign of recognition.

"Hi, I'm Jerry Jeff Walker."

The performer's eyes widened like he had just been stuck in the rear with a cattle prod—shocked into the adjoining Louisiana parish. "Ah, well, ah...." He fumbled for words. "I didn't mean any disrespect," he explained. "Must have been someone else who said he was you that taught me the way to sing that song. Hope it was okay."

"No problem," soothed Jerry Jeff. "I appreciate you singing it. Maybe I'll get some royalties out of this club. Or at least a free drink."

The singer laughed nervously, then wandered backstage, shaking his head, and, no doubt, vowing never again to use that line about Jerry Jeff.

Walker returned to his bar mates and ordered an extra round for us. Toad, a railroad buff whose enthusiasm for riding trains equaled mine, huddled with Jimmy, hatching a plan to take a train back to Nashville.

"But I'm going to Mobile to see some people," Jimmy told Toad.

"It'd be a blast if all of us took the train to Nashville. You can go to Mobile anytime, Jimmy."

"Okay," surrendered Buffett, an easy convert to nocturnal, alcohol-fueled changes of latitudes and changes of attitudes. They would now work on Jerry Jeff to lure him into the trip.

"I'd love to," Jerry Jeff responded to the invitation. "But I'm flying to Los Angeles tomorrow to talk to some folks about some movie music."

"Are you sure?" Toad pressed. "It's the *Pan American*, the train that the Louisville and Nashville Railroad is discontinuing. This will be your last chance to ride it. One of America's last great trains."

"It's a big business deal in L.A. My manager would be mad if I stiffed those guys."

"Are you really sure?" Jimmy echoed Toad's plea. "You can stay with my wife and me—we've got a neat log cabin in Nashville with plenty of room. We can write some songs together on the train and in Nashville, then you can go on to Los Angeles."

Jerry Jeff stirred his drink, took a big gulp, and thought about the offer for another three seconds before responding, "Sounds like fun. What time does it leave?"

"It departs at exactly 5:15 in the afternoon from the New Orleans station, goes through Mississippi and Alabama and arrives in Nashville at 8:50 the next morning," rattled off Toad, a walking railroad timetable. "It's got sleepers, coaches and a diner, so we can have dinner and breakfast on it."

Now it was Walker's turn to evangelize one final rider as the attention turned to me, the only holdout. I had driven the 200 miles from Nashville to Memphis and rode the Illinois Central's fabled streamliner *City of New Orleans* to its namesake destination.

"How about you?" he asked me.

"I sure would if my car wasn't in Memphis," I argued. "It'd be crazy to take the train to Nashville when my car's in Memphis. I'm leaving on the *City of New Orleans* north to Memphis at seven in the morning."

"Oh, come on, Gerry," pestered Toad, adding a land-lord/tenant slant to his plea. "If you don't go with us, I won't pay my rent."

"You don't pay it anyway."

Jerry Jeff and Jimmy laughed as Toad contemplated alternative methods of changing my mind. I didn't find out until later, after the statute of limitations dissipated into history, that he joined my other companions in a conspiracy to drop odd little pills into my rum and Cokes. I slowly became fuzzy-brained, time melted into a meaningless measuring device and my world dissolved into a dull blur of dim sight and loud sound.

Three o'clock had turned into four and nudged five o'clock as we staggered down Royal Street where one of us, to this day I'm not sure which one, had a room at the Cornstalk Fence Hotel. Four of us squeezed within a claustrophobic single bedroom. What remained of my senses battled their fragile logic as the pressure mounted.

"You certainly don't want to sleep only one hour," Toad the train guru said. "You'll feel awful when you wake up."

"You'll be a wreck," Jimmy stressed.

"Hey, you can borrow Jimmy's car and drive from Nashville to Memphis to get your car," plotted Jerry Jeff, throwing Buffett's car into the already baffling multi-mode transportation mix without gaining any prior approval from the owner.

A heavy mental curtain, thick as the maroon Bijou Theatre drapery, swept closed across my beleaguered brain. My theatre lights were about to be dimmed. Show over. The room began spinning and I fell face first into a pillow with my last words a muffled, "Seven o'clock."

I dreamed of trains early that morning, and my vision included a train whistle that must have blown around 7 a.m.: the Memphis-bound *City of New Orleans*, minus one confirmed passenger. When I awoke in the afternoon, my only choice demanded I join this hung-over crew of crazed music-makers for their excursion back to Nashville.

"Hey, Gerry," Jerry Jeff said. "Toad has got us rooms in a Pullman car, including two double bedrooms. He says we can open the partitions and have a jam session all night long."

An elephant sat on my head, or at least it felt like an elephant. Could have been a rhinoceros. "Ohhh, please, I'm going to grab dinner on it and sleep all the way to Nashville. Don't let me over-sleep this time or I'll end up in Cincinnati."

My eyes tried to focus on the room that looked much better when it was blurred. Clothing hung from light fixtures while clumps of underwear and long-suffering socks, stuck to each other, formed malodorous mounds on the floor. "God, what happened in here? Did we have a tornado come through in the middle of the night?"

"Don't know," Jimmy said. "We were asleep."

"Not too much is broken," Jerry Jeff reasoned in a tone that always seemed to make sense of bizarre situations. He took inventory. "A couple lamps appear to be a little demolished. Buffett smashed the radio when it played John Denver. And don't walk in the bathroom barefooted or look in the toilet."

Jimmy peered under the bed for his shirt, while Jerry Jeff reached atop the dresser mirror for his pants. Buried deep in concentration, Toad studied the April 26, 1970 edition of the thin Louisville and Nashville Railroad passenger train timetable. I could have sworn he was drooling with anticipation as he kept wiping the corners of his mouth with a formerly white handkerchief.

Only hours earlier, Jimmy was bound for Alabama, Toad for Texas, Jerry Jeff for California, and me for Memphis, Tennessee. Now we were all headed for the same destination—Nashville.

This I knew was going to be an experience.

Phoneward Bound

"We'll need to leave here at 4:30 to drop off the rental car and get to the train in time," directed Travel Agent Toad. "Everybody hear that?"

If Jerry Jeff heard it, he certainly didn't remember it. After putting on pants, T-shirt and shoes, he rambled out the door headed for God knows where. "I'll be back," he promised.

"Jerry Jeff probably knows a lot of people here," Toad conjectured. "I hope he gets back in time. Let's go get something to drink."

"How about Café du Monde for coffee and beignets," I suggested, a reasonable choice, I thought. Toad and Buffett quickly shot down the suggestion.

"What are you, some sort of tourist?" quizzed Jimmy. "Jesus, it's afternoon. You're in New Orleans, man. Toad's not talking about coffee. I know a place where we can find the best Bloody Mary in town. It's over by that cemetery where Marie Laveau is buried. We can put a mark on her grave before we leave. We'll need extra good luck if Jerry Jeff comes along."

Jimmy picked up the phone and called his wife Margie back in Nashville, a chat that immediately had him on the defensive. The Jimmy end of the conversation went like this:

"Yes, honey, I know they were expecting me in Mobile.

"Yes, Margie, I'm sure they will, but they'll get over it.

"Oh, I forgot about the birthday. I'll make it up somehow.

"Gerry and I ran into Toad Andrews last night. He's coming with us, so notify Nancy to meet him at Union Station. And Gerry's coming with us, too. Tell Ellen, so she'll know.

"She's there? Spent the night? I'll tell Gerry. Yes. Yes."

Jimmy cupped the phone and whispered to me a question relayed to Margie from my wife. "Ellen wants to know why you're taking the train to Nashville when your car's in Memphis."

Suddenly, *I* wanted to know the answer to the very same question, too. "Tell her I'm going to drive your car from Nashville to Memphis to get my car." I somehow remembered that plan through the fog of the previous night.

"Margie, he's going to drive our car over to Memphis so he can get his car and return home."

The only sounds I heard from Margie's end of the discussion sizzled out of the phone like electricity zinging on a hot wire: "He's going to *whaaat?* Not in *my* car! Who's going to drive it back?"

Jimmy looked perplexed and tried to rub some of the sleep away from his face and finger-comb the hopeless tangle of his long brown and dirty-blond hair that cascaded to his shoulders. No one had previously thought out the plan to its logical conclusion if, indeed, it had one. His brain wasn't up to speed yet in dealing with Margie's persistent inquisition.

"That is a good, legitimate question that I didn't deal with last night," I whispered to Jimmy as he split his attention between an increasingly agitated wife and an increasingly confused me.

"Yes, I realize if Gerry drives our car…okay, okay, *your* car…to Memphis, he will have *two* cars in Memphis when he arrives there. This is obviously something we're going to have to figure out while we're on the train.

"Oh, I'm bringing someone with me, at least I think I am. Guess who I met yesterday?

"No, not Frankie Ford, for God's sake! Why would I bring *him* home? Gerry introduced me to Jerry Jeff Walker at the college. He was on the bill with me.

"Yes, the show went great. The entire audience loved it.

"No, he's not a professor. The guy that wrote 'Mr. Bojangles.' What a trip he is. If he shows up before the train leaves, he's coming with us. We might write some songs together. Can you imagine that?

"What? Where else? At our place. We have that extra couch. I told him he could stay with us.

"Well, I'm sorry. I'm letting you know now. It's not the last minute.

"No, he's a great guy. You'll love him. He's real cool. He seems to like Wild Turkey a lot. Do you think you could…

"No, no, no. You don't have to cook a turkey dinner, for Christ's sake. It's something you drink. Whiskey. Don't worry about food—I've been with him for over twenty-four hours and I haven't seen him eat anything yet.

"No, I stayed away from the stuff. I just drank rum. Actually, we turned in kind of early last night.

"No, he's not bringing a band. It's just him, honey. It's no big deal. You'll like him.

"I promise we'll be there when the train arrives in Union Station tomorrow morning. Toad has already booked us reservations in a sleeper. It'll be our last chance to ride the *Pan American*. The damn L and N Railroad is killing it. Bastards—all they care about is hauling freight. Bring a camera."

"What? What does Valentine's Day have to do with this?"

I cringed when Jimmy repeated "Valentine's Day." Obviously, still a sore spot with Margie, and, probably Ellen, Jimmy and I had impulsively hopped aboard a train for what we had planned as a quick single-day round-trip ride from Nashville to Louisville and back. We promised our wives that we would be back in Nashville at 7 p.m. in time for our Valentine's Day dinner celebration. During that snowy and frigid February day, we harbored the best of intentions to work on our screenplay *The Quitters* while enjoying the ride through the beautiful Tennessee and Kentucky snowscapes along the route, worthy of Currier & Ives treatment.

Unfortunately, we worked harder on a full bottle of rum than on the writing project and were quite looped by the time Louisville arrived. That's where we made a simple mistake that resulted in later difficulties. We forgot to get off. The train—yes, our friend the *Pan American* again—was now rumbling down the snowy tracks somewhere between Louisville and the terminal city of Cincinnati before we knew what had happened. We were traveling toward Cincinnati on the road and toward trouble at home.

Jimmy and I had returned to the rapidly diminishing supply of rum and made an emergency purchase of all remaining liquor bottles in the lounge-diner before it closed early. We attempted some half-hearted crude efforts at writing as our train crawled toward Cincinnati several hours late for its anticipated 5:35 p.m. arrival. In honest retrospect, I can't state that we finished one paragraph worth retention. And then there was the matter of finding lodging in Cincinnati on a snowy night.

"Don't worry," Jimmy said. "My friend Ricky Bennett lives in Cincinnati. We'll stay with him tonight and head back to Nashville in the morning. I just wish the dining car was open. I'm starving."

Jimmy and I must have been living right. No sooner had he spoken about the complete absence of food on the train than the *Pan American* shuddered sharply with a bang and the brakes squealed in an emergency stop.

"What the hell?" Jimmy said, looking out the window. "Oh, lord, we hit a station wagon!"

No damage to the train, but the front of the station wagon was crunched into a jagged ball of metal, chrome and glass. By the time the famished Buffett and I slipped off the train to view the accident, the driver had been rushed to the hospital, banged up, bruised and bloody, but at least not dead.

We peered into the back seat of the vehicle and discovered the reason for the driver's trip through this perilous icy weather. There, covered with the wrecked jetsam and flotsam of a formidable train-car collision was a 16-inch cardboard pizza container.

"He's certainly not going to eat that tonight," Jimmy reasoned, staring with hunger at the inviting pizza.

"And people in China are starving, not to mention us," I agreed.

While the police and train engineer sorted through details of the grade crossing accident, Jimmy reached in the back seat, scraped shards of glass off the top of the box, shoved it inside his coat and we snuck our meal back on board. The pizza was still warm, and disappeared in seconds.

That was the good news. The bad news was going to be the call from Cincinnati to Nashville to notify two wives who anxiously awaited our arrival in time for Valentine's Day dinner that we would now be celebrating a day late if they were still talking to us. We argued over who had to make the call, then flipped a coin. I won. Jimmy lost. He called when we finally reached the Cincinnati station near midnight.

They had a fiery phone conversation if there ever was one. "But Margie" this and "but Margie" that—a litany of "but Margies" until she had finished with her husband and demanded to talk to me. I had time for only one "but Margie" before she tore into me with her threat, "And for you, Gerry Wood, if you two ever get back to Nashville, I'm going to get Ellen to make you do the dishes for a whole month!"

Somehow, despite the impending gloom of a month-long kitchen patrol punishment meted out by Ellen, via Margie, I felt I would be getting off easier than my co-writing partner once he dared return home.

That's why I had cringed when Margie brought up "Valentine's Day," during still another Buffett phone call involving Jimmy, me, trains, and altered plans.

"No, this has nothing to do with last Valentine's Day," Jimmy continued his conversation from the Cornstalk Fence Hotel in New Orleans. "That was a fluke of nature. I promise you, we'll be there right on time tomorrow morning. Which means, I'd better start packing right now."

For the first time there was silence on the other end of the line. Jimmy took that as a good sign. "Well, I love you Margie. I've got to go to church now before we leave," he joked. "I'd better take a bath in the holy water. See you at Union Station in the morning. Bye, baby."

Jimmy hung up the phone and said to me, in flat resignation, a refrain I was to hear often during our travels together: "I think we're in trouble again."

"Yeah," I nodded in groggy affirmation. "Let's find that Bloody Mary place. Do they make doubles?"

On the (Rail)Road Again

A portrait of impatience in action, Toad Andrews nervously stalked our room at the Cornstalk Fence Hotel at 4:59 p.m. "Where is he? Where's Jerry Jeff? We've got sixteen minutes to make our train. We've gotta leave now!"

Just as we tossed our worldly possessions into the trunk of the rental car, Jerry Jeff ambled leisurely up the street. "Where you going?" he asked.

"Get in!" Toad demanded. "The train now! We're going to miss it!"

"Where's my guitar?"

"In the trunk. Get in."

I angled the car through the narrow streets of the French Quarter, reached Canal Street and took a sharp right. Toad was counting down the minutes like a boxing match referee timing a knockdown. Nine. Eight. Seven. Six. Five.

"Hey, stop here!" Jerry Jeff commanded as we passed a liquor store on Canal.

"We don't have time," informed Toad, sweat pouring off his reddened face and down his neck due to the suffocating humidity, thick enough to slice with a butcher knife, and the nerve-shattering attempt to catch the train. "Four minutes and it's gone."

"I'm not getting on any train without a bottle of Wild Turkey," Jerry Jeff stated in that calm voice of reasoning, not to be denied or averted. "No way."

I slammed to a stop. Jerry Jeff ran into the store and—timed by Toad's gold-plated railroad watch—emerged with a grin on his face and two large bottles of Wild Turkey in his arms.

"That took a minute and twenty-seven seconds," Toad told Walker, hauling him and the loot into the back seat.

"Is that a new world's record for the Booze-Buying Olympics?" asked Jerry Jeff.

"Did I win the gold or the silver?" He lovingly patted the bottles of mahogany-colored firewater. "I've got the *bronze* here. That's all that counts."

"Two minutes!" Toad shouted, not interested in color-coded frivolity until safely aboard the train. I tore off down Canal to Loyola Avenue. "Left on Loyola. Run that red light!" he barked.

After a quick scan for police, pedestrians and oncoming traffic, I followed Toad's instructions and shot through the stoplight with a screeching left turn. We pulled into the drive in front of the train station with one minute left. "I've got to turn in the car," I told him.

"No time left. Leave it here. We'll take care of that later."

A mad scramble through the station, out the gate and down the platform gained impetus and speed as the conductor yelled, "All aboard!"

The bizarre band looked like the tattered remnants of a Chinese New Year's dragon parade, half running, half staggering to the side of the Pullman car while lugging critical life-support carry-on items such as two guitars and two bottles of Wild Turkey, plus a case of beer Jimmy rescued from the trunk. Whistle blowing, the train lurched forward as we jumped aboard, Toad shoving us up the steps.

Toad ran along the platform as the train picked up speed and he tried to catch it. Had *we* made the train while leaving *him* behind, suicide would have been his only alternative. Just as the train was about to slip out of his grasp, Toad looked up and saw a familiar helping hand reach out of the vestibule doorway to pull him up the steep steps.

"Well, Mr. Andrews, so nice to have you aboard again," the gray-haired, black porter greeted him, hauling Toad aboard.

"Thanks, Mr. Wins," Toad said, wiping that formerly white handkerchief over his face and mouth, the absorbent powers rendered useless now because of the soggy nature of the drenched cloth. "I want you to meet my friends."

A Song is Born, a Woman Scorned

The train rattled across bridges and trestles, gliding past Bay St. Louis and Pass Christian as we wolfed down dinner in the diner—a meal made yummier for some of our group thanks to the odors of burning hemp that still lingered back in the sleeper like Exhibit A evidence. Well fed after a delicious roast beef dinner topped off by apple pie a la mode, all washed down with two bottles of wine, we lurched down the narrow aisles to the Pullman car and settled into our quarters. Mr. Wins had opened adjoining bedroom compartment doors, creating a large suite on wheels for us.

Bracketed by bottles of beer and booze, and enjoying the hypnotic motion of the train, Toad, Jimmy and Jerry Jeff opened their guitar cases and began an impromptu concert on the rails. Toad, safe and sound aboard his element, relaxed for the first time since the train trip to Nashville turned from plan to reality.

Jimmy tried out one of his new songs, "Captain America," then Jerry Jeff followed with one of his beautiful ballads. Jimmy countered with a recently completed composition that demonstrated his songwriting genius and early potential, "Livingston's Gone to Texas."

After midnight and the fourth warning from the shushing conductor who patrolled with Police Academy paranoia and persistence, Wild Turkey escalated to a rank high on the endangered species list. That sent us into missions within our baggage to renew the sources of altering moods. The Pullman performance continued.

Somewhere in the middle of the night, in the middle of Mississippi, or it might have been Alabama, the conductor threatened to throw us off the train. Had he carried out the threat, we would have been prime fodder for extended lodgings in god-awful, bleak, baking small town Southern jails. Multiple offense, prison-primed, long-haired, short-fused, loud-mouthed hippies just ripe and ready for the redneck gendarmes after they probed through our assorted luggage and marched us off to hoosegow justice.

"Keep the noise down, keep the racket down," he dictated. "Nobody on this car can sleep."

"There's nobody else on this car except us," Toad pointed out. "I've checked out every room."

"Hell, keep it down anyway," L&N's finest instructed. "The engineer can't even hear his damn whistle."

Jerry Jeff defused the situation by giving the Hitleresque conductor what was left in the Wild Turkey bottle. As Jerry Jeff described our New Orleans romp and train trip in his fascinating no-holds-barred autobiography *Gypsy Songman*: "In the course of the day, we absorbed numerous varying reprimands about proper behavior on a train. The conductor took a few nips of our Wild Turkey and spent more time in our compartment than anywhere else."

Now the *Pan American* picked up speed, rocketing along the rails. Jerry Jeff paused before beginning his next number.

"Hey, I've got an idea for a song." He strummed a C, F and G on his guitar, and began, "She's a railroad lady, just a little bit shady, she spent her whole life on the train."

Jimmy's eyes lit up at the song's introduction, and he

quickly chorded his guitar in tune with the melody, and added, "She's a semi-good looker, but the fast rails they took her. Now she's trying, just trying to get home again."

The song was coming together.

"What's the name of the station in Boston?" Jerry Jeff asked.

"There's two stations," answered Toad, king of railroad trivia. "North Station and South Station. Take your pick."

Without missing a beat, Jerry Jeff crooned, "South Station in Boston to the freight yards of Austin, from the Florida sunshine to the New Orleans rain...."

Jimmy diverted the lady's story toward a tragic turn as he improvised, "Once a Pullman car traveler, now the brakeman won't have her, she's trying, just trying to get home again."

My contribution came when Jimmy and Jerry Jeff reached the end of the line on a verse. "How's this, guys?" I offered, though I felt naked without a guitar and songwriting credentials in this room full of supreme talents and master pickers. "Once a highballing loner thought he could own her...." In later years after the song had been recorded by Willie Nelson, Merle Haggard and others, I would kid Jerry Jeff and Jimmy about my "missing" royalties due for supplying one small segment. "Yeah," Jerry Jeff would say, "that was probably worth about two hundred bucks."

Jimmy followed my lead with, "He bought her a fur coat and a big diamond ring."

Eyes closed, Jerry Jeff smiled and sang, "She hocked them for cold cash, left town on the Wabash."

"Not thinking, not thinking of home way back then," Jimmy continued the tuneful tale.

All of us sang the chorus—"She's a railroad lady, just a little bit shady..." It worked!

Exhausted by the song-birthing process, we left it at that—an unfinished country symphony, Number One. A few days later, back in Nashville, Jimmy would add a final verse about how the railroad lady headed back home to Kentucky on a bus because of what Steve Goodman, described in "City of New Orleans" as "the disappearing railroad blues." Jerry Jeff never liked that climax, but at least it was finally finished, and another song was delivered naked and screaming into the world.

Before we left the master bedroom suite for our own roomettes, Toad asked Jerry Jeff if he would sing "Mr. Bojangles," a risky request since many singers dread performing their biggest hits. Roger Miller hated to sing "King of the Road." Joe South would rather vomit than labor through "Walk a Mile in My Shoes" for the millionth time.

But Jerry Jeff was not, and is not, Roger Miller or Joe South. "Sure," he said.

And, rocking to the rhythm of the rails, Walker sang his immortal story about a black man, his dancing shoes and his dog that he grieves for after twenty years. Outside the windows, dim yellow stars of farm lights broke the darkness in the distance, sliding by in silence.

"I knew a man, Bojangles, and he'd dance for you. In worn-out shoes…"

While in New Orleans, Jerry Jeff had pointed out the jail where he had the good fortune to be incarcerated in the same cell as the sepia gypsy who gave him the inspiration for the song. "Every now and then," Walker explained, "the cops sweep the streets of all the drunks to make their arrest records look better. That's how he and I ended up there together. And he started telling me about his life. It sure changed *my* life!"

"Mr. Bojangles, Mr. Bojangles. Dance."

Jerry Jeff had belted out Bojangles thousands of times before, in rowdy, rotgut bars and crowded concerts. But this night, with the clickety-clack of the train wheels as his personal metronome, he graced the tale with freshness and force as though it were the debut unveiling of a new masterpiece.

His fingers pressed deeply into the struts, his face grew flushed, the veins in his neck bulged. And he sang the last verse.

When he finished, the Pullman room was quiet except for the mournful sounds of a train on its last run. All of us were in absolute awe of the goosebump prodding performance of a perfect song by its imperfect author. A gang of previously raucous railroad rabble-rousers had been reduced to zero decibels by the immense talent of one of the planet's premier talents.

Nothing could surpass, or follow, this performance on this special night, a movable feast for the ears and eyes.

Elegy for a Friend

The L&N's *Pan American* surged northward, wailing its own sad version of the disappearing railroad blues, its whistle crying at the crossings, fading into the blackness that would soon give way to the virgin light of dawn. These tracks would soon be minus the magic of railroad travel, train whistles in the night, passengers trying to sleep in awkward positions on coach seats, slumbering peacefully on Pullman beds, sharing drinks with strangers in the lounge, eating breakfast in the diner with its aromatic blend of coffee and bacon, watching America pass by in a slow and memorable panorama that would be gone forever—a haunting and sorrowful thought.

But "Railroad Lady" and "Mr. Bojangles" dispatched the *Pan American* into history with a flourish fit for a king, a tribute worthy of a queen. The train sought Nashville, and then would press onward to the final stop at the station with a name sadly appropriate for this last journey before oblivion—Cincinnati Union *Terminal.*

Without a word, Jimmy Buffett, Toad Andrews and I headed for our rooms on the night-turned-to-morning that "Railroad Lady" was born, "Mr. Bojangles" was resurrected and our friend died.

Our beloved train pal, the *Pan American*, had provided us with her own swan song.

As if we didn't already know, we learned once again that it all begins with a song.

And, this time, it also ended with a song.

Chapter 15

Tales from Chet Atkins and Garrison Keillor

Maestro of the guitar, Chet Atkins also achieved fame as one of the architects of the Nashville Sound. His work wandered the country and pop charts, and he was as comfortable performing in front of a big-city symphony orchestra as he was picking for a small country band. As a studio musician, producer and RCA Records vice president, Chet steered the country sound down smoother roads, adding strings and Anita Kerr-style background harmonies that gained new legions of listeners for the de-twanged product, while turning off some traditional country purists in the process.

Chet was the gentlest of men, and, though a shyness and soft-spoken quality glazed his persona, he could charm a snake out of the bushes with his smile and sense of humor—dry as a bone and funny as hell. During a roast honoring Porter Wagoner, Atkins announced,

"They had a tornado out there in Porter's hometown of West Plains, Missouri, and it did one hundred thousand dollars' worth of improvements."

I once had the opportunity to sit and talk to my two favorite guitarists—Chet Atkins and Mark Knopfler. They had just finished recording an album together that included their heartwarming ode to friendship, "The Next Time I'm in Town." Unknown to Chet, he had been an early mentor to the British rock star who powered Dire Straits to the top. Mark reflected some of Chet's traits and talents: a sense of shyness, modesty, and incomparable low-keyed guitar virtuosity. Knopfler could sing a ring around Chet, but Mr. Atkins still out-dueled him on the frets.

The day before Independence Day 2001, music lovers and friends packed the Ryman Auditorium in Nashville, to mourn the loss of Chet Atkins and celebrate the life of this remarkable artist who had elevated his music from the hills of Tennessee to faraway peaks. Bereaved country stars paid homage to the fallen master as the Ryman threatened to be transformed into the Temple of Gloom. Close friend Eddy Arnold broke down in tears at the podium, his strong resonance reduced to a sob and a whisper.

Then a familiar figure—in voice, not appearance—strode on stage to salute his departed creative comrade, Garrison Keillor. He's the gentle genius who provides the only contemporary lifeline to America's golden era of radio back when folks gathered around crystal sets, battery-powered devices and deluxe console models to enjoy mental theater far more compelling and realistic than anything offered today on the medium that supplanted its drama and comedy—television. Long gone are Jack Benny's trips with Rochester down the stairs to his dungeon-like basement, Fibber McGee's avalanching closet, the mush-mush-you-huskies icy adventures of Sergeant Preston and Yukon King, the stirring theme from *The Lone Ranger*, the chilling presence of *The Shadow*, and the off-the-wall comical skits of Bob Elliot and Ray Goulding. But no interpreter of the idiom arrives better equipped to nurture the flickering flame of those audio-only days than Keillor with his weekly National Public Radio program, *A Prairie Home Companion.*

Ironically, Keillor's inspiration for the show came years earlier on the same Ryman stage where he now stood. He had visited the *Grand Ole Opry* for the music. He left with a mission. This grand ol' Mecca of memories welcomed a man equal in talent with those who graced it before him: Roy Acuff, Minnie Pearl, Bill Monroe, Hank Williams, Ernest Tubb, Kitty Wells, Marty Robbins, Patsy Cline, Loretta Lynn, Porter Wagoner, Dolly Parton, Bill Anderson, Little Jimmy Dickens...

Enter, stage right, the unannounced native from the unknown and mysterious north country of Minnesota who would offer some praise for his brother in the perilous blood-kinship of those who dare heed the alluring and addictive promises from untrustworthy gods that prod, and sometimes destroy, the truly gifted. Brick by brick, Keillor rebuilt riverboat captain Tom Ryman's tabernacle into a well-grounded and fitting embarkation point for Chet's sendoff.

Keillor's majestic and mesmerizing tones graced the grand hall as he began the most stirring and poignant speech that anyone fortunate enough to be in the Ryman at that moment will ever hear. As a friend of the man and a fan of the music, he painted a rich, lustrous, warts-and-all portrait of the artist as a young, and old, man.

Garrison Keillor graciously gave me permission to include this tribute. It starts with a "Dear Garrison" letter from Chet and ends with a gentle flourish from Garrison.

One of his most brilliant observations was: "If Chet was a fan of yours, you never needed another one."

Those who heard these plaudits, and were aware of Chet's fondness for him, realized that Garrison Keillor will never need another fan.

Dear Garrison,

I went up home to east Tennessee the other day. I was invited, went and saw a dozen folks that I hadn't seen in 45 or 50 years. Every damn one of them said, "I'll bet you don't know who I am," etc. I admitted I didn't and they seemed disappointed. I left there when I had just turned 11. I received an award for just growing up there, I suppose, and I couldn't think of one nice thing to say. Those were some of the worst years of the old man's life, don't you know. But even the bad ones are good now that I think about it.

Back to the sunny side of life, I played New Bedford, Mass. last Saturday and did very well. I am warmer in the provinces, don't you know. I had a screamer in the audience. Saw her later and she wasn't all that bad, about thirty-five, a feller could run some of that weight off of her and maybe fall in love. Some of the folks had been to my other shows, tho, because when I went into my ad libs, it seemed like they had heard it all before. Anyway I got some bifocal contact lenses the other day for when performing. This morning I got the left one in in about ten seconds, the other one took thirty minutes. I kept jabbing it in my eye and the damn thing kept sticking to my finger. I expect the people to audibly say, "Who is that young cock up there?" Or I may hear them say, "How does a man his age see to play without specs?" Anyway, when I got on the plane in Boston, I went to the toilet and get some Kleenex. Well, I opened the door and there sat a lady on the john. I took the time to say, "Oh, excuse me" (why, I don't know) and got the hell out of there. I'm

*still embarrassed and it wasn't my fault. This has happened to
me three times since 1942 and every time it has been a lady.
Well, I probably have walked in on men, but that is so un-
eventful. Anyway, I went back to my seat and composed a per-
sonals ad: "Former star with youthful body and only slight loss
of hair, is athletic and enjoys listening to country music, especially his own recordings, desires to meet young beautiful twenty-
year-old star. Females only please." Maybe you could use it on
your show.*

> *As ever,*
> *Chet*

It's fitting to meet here at the Ryman because it was
here, on a Saturday night in the summer of 1946, Red Foley
came on The Grand Ole Opry and sang "Old Shep" and
then, before the commercial break for Prince Albert in a
can, nodded to his guitarist and said, "Ladies and gentlemen, Mr. Chester Atkins will now play 'Maggie' on the
acoustic guitar," and Mr. Atkins did, and afterward Minnie
Pearl came up and kissed him and said, "You're a wonderful
musician, you're just what we've been needing around here."

He played guitar in a style that hadn't been seen before,
with a thumb pick for the bass note and two fingers to play
the contrapuntal melody, and at a time when guitarists were
expected to be flashy and play "Under the Double Eagle"
with the guitar up behind their head, this one hunched down
over the guitar and made it sing, made a melody line that
was beautiful and legato. A woman wrote, who saw him
play in a roadhouse in Cincinnati in 1946, "He sat hunched
in the spotlight and played and the whole room suddenly
got quiet. It was a drinking and dancing crowd, but there
was something about Chet Atkins that could take your breath
away."

Chester Burton Atkins was born June 20, 1924, the son of Ida Sharp and James Arley Atkins, a music teacher and piano tuner and singer, near Luttrell, Tennessee, on the farm of his grandfather, who fought on the Union side in the Civil War.

Chet was born into a mess of trouble: His people were poor, his folks split up when he was six, he suffered from asthma, he grew up lonely and scared, tongue-tied and shy. His older brothers played music and he listened and when he was six, he got a ukulele. When he broke a string, he pulled a wire off the screen door and tuned it up. He took up the guitar when he was nine, a Sears Silvertone with the action about a half-inch high at the 12th fret, torture to play. He'd tune it up to a major chord and play it with a kitchen knife for a slide, Hawaiian style, "Steel Guitar Rag." When he was 11, he went to live with his daddy in Columbus, Georgia, where on a summer day you could see the snake tracks in the dust on a dirt road, but at night the radio brought in Cincinnati and Atlanta and Knoxville and even New York City.

That was the music that spoke to his heart.

Chet got a lot of music from his dad, who was a trained singer—the old hymns and sentimental ballads, which Chet remembered all his life—he could sing you several verses of "In the Gloaming" or "Seeing Nellie Home," whether you asked for them or not—and he knew the fiddle tunes and mountain music that he picked up trying to play the fiddle—but on the radio he heard music that really entranced him, that was freer and looser and more jangly and elegant and attitudinous. His brother Jim played rhythm guitar with Les Paul when Les was with Fred Waring and His Pennsylvanians and Chet paid close attention to that, and to George Barnes and the Sons of the Pioneers and the Hoosier Hot

Shots, and Merle Travis who he heard on a crystal set from WLW in Cincinnati. (Merle was a big hero of his and he named his daughter Merle; luckily for her, Chet didn't feel so strongly about Riley Puckett or Low Stokes or Gid Tanner.) Chet tried to get the Merle Travis sound, and in the process, he came up with his own, and then he discovered Django Reinhardt and that set something loose in him.

You might be shy and homely and puny and from the sticks and feel looked down upon, but if you could play the guitar like that, you would be aristocracy and never have to point it out, anybody with sense would know it and the others don't matter anyway.

He met Django backstage once in Chicago when Django was touring with Duke Ellington and got his autograph. Chet said, "I wanted to play for him but I didn't get the chance." But in Knoxville, doing the Midday Merry Go Round, he met Homer and Jethro, Henry Haynes and Kenneth Burns, who were hip to Django too and on Chet's wavelength and in 1949 they made an instrumental album called "Galloping Guitar"—sort of the Hot Club of Nashville. It got some airplay, and that was his first big success and he was on his way.

Chet had dropped out of high school to go into radio and the music business—first with Jumping Bill Carlisle and Archie Campbell in Knoxville, and Johnnie & Jack in Raleigh, then Red Foley in Chicago and Springfield, Missouri, and Mother Maybelle and the Carter Sisters. In Cincinnati, he met Leona Johnson, who was singing on WLW with her twin sister Lois, and after a year of courtship they married in 1946. He wrote in 1984: "Our percolator went out the other day and we counted up…she has stayed with me through four of them. If I were her, I wouldn't have stayed around through the first one, which was a non-electric. After drinking coffee, there would be a residue on the cup and folks would read it and tell your fortune. Anyway, she is mine and she is a winner."

Chet got himself fired plenty of times along the way, a badge of honor for a musician with a mind of his own, and he kept getting fired in an upward direction and wound up coming to Nashville and WSM and the Opry and RCA, under the patronage of Fred Rose and Steve Sholes. He got to see the end of the era of the medicine show and the hillbilly band with the comedian with the blacked-out teeth and the beginnings of rock 'n' roll—Chet had a front-row seat, as the guitarist, and he remembered everything he saw and he knew stories about a lot of people in this room that are not in your official press packets. In his recollections, he was kind but he was honest, like the bartender in *Frankie and Johnny*—"I don't want to cause you no trouble, but I ain't gonna tell you no lies."

This was a man who knew the icons close-up—he could talk about Hank Williams and Elvis and Patsy Cline and Mother Maybelle Carter and who they really were and what was on their minds and what they ate for breakfast. He knew so many giants.

This man was a giant himself. He was the guitar player of the 20th century. He was the model of who you should be and what you should look like. You could tell it whenever he picked up a guitar, the way it fit him. His upper body was shaped to it, from a lifetime of playing: his back was slightly hunched, his shoulders rounded, and the guitar was the missing piece. He was an artist, and there was no pretense in him; he never waved the flag or held up the cross or traded on his own sorrows. He was the guitarist. His humor was self-deprecating; he was his own best critic. He inspired all sorts of players who never played anything like him. He was generous and admired other players' work and he told them so. He had a natural reserve to him, but when he admired people, he went all out to tell them about it. And because there was no deception in him, his praise meant more than just about anything else. If Chet was a fan of yours, you never needed another one.

He was not a saint. He was a restless man. He'd be in a room and then he'd need to be somewhere else. He had deep moods that came and went and that he couldn't enunciate. He had a certain harmless vanity to him. There was an album cover late in his career with a picture air brushed to make him look about 23 that we had to kid him about. He liked synthesizers more than he maybe ought to have. He sometimes kicked his golf ball to improve his lie.

When he was almost fifty, he had a stroke of good luck, when he got colon cancer and thought he was going to die, and when he didn't die, he found a whole new love of life. He walked away from the corporate music world and fell in love with the guitar again and went all over performing with Paul Yandell, playing with all the great orchestras, notably the Boston Pops, and started living by his own clock, so he had time to sit and talk with people and pick music with them and enjoy the social side of music and have more fun. "I haven't learned to exercise the right of privacy," he said. "Folks are always calling and I drop everything and entertain them." He had a gift for friendship. He was so generous with stories. Some of us are able to impersonate storytellers, but Chet was the real thing, and if you drove around Nashville with him, he remembered one after another; it was a documentary movie about country music. Chet loved so many people. He especially loved the ones who seemed a little wild to him and who made him laugh. He loved his grandkids Jonathan and Amanda and talked them up every

Billboard *Nashville Bureau Chief Gerry Wood presents* Billboard *Country Awards to Chet Atkins, left, and RCA Nashville head Jerry Bradley. (Photo courtesy of Gerry Wood)*

chance he got, though I don't know how wild they were. Dolly Parton always made him laugh, the way she flirted with him. A few months ago, she came to see him, he was in bed, dying, and she made him laugh for about an hour, telling him things I'm not about to repeat here. He loved Waylon Jennings. He loved Lenny Breaux. Jerry Reed. Ray Stevens. Vince Gill. Steve Wariner. And Brother Dave Gardner, the hipster revivalist comedian whom Chet discovered doing stand-up in a Nashville club between sets as a drummer and who said, "Dear hearts, gathered here to rejoice in the glorious Southland. Joy to the world! The South has always been the South. And I believe the only reason that folks live in the north is because they have jobs up there."

He loved doing shows. He never had a bad night. He played some notes he didn't mean to play, but they never were bad notes. They simply were other notes. He was such a professional it was hard to bug him, but I succeeded when we did a show together and at the end I took his hand and we took a bow together. The next night, he said to me before the show, "Don't take my hand on stage that way; you know what people will think, you being a northern liberal and all." I found that during the bow I could make him flinch just by gesturing toward him.

He liked to be alone backstage. He liked it quiet and calm in the dressing room and he counted on George Lunn to make it that way. I remember him backstage, alone, walking around in the cavernous dark of some opera house out west, holding the guitar, playing, singing to himself; he needed to be alone with himself and get squared away, because the Chet people saw on stage was the same Chet you hung around with in his office, joking with Paul about having a swimming pool shaped like a guitar amp, the joke about "By the time I learned I couldn't tune very well, I was too rich to care," and singing "Would Jesus Wear A Rolex," and "I Just Can't Say Goodbye" and ending the show with his ravishing beautiful solo, "Vincent," the audience sitting in rapt silence. It was all the same Chet who sat at home with Leona, watching a golf tournament with the sound off, and playing his guitar, a long stream-of-consciousness medley in which twenty or thirty tunes came together perfectly, as in a dream, his daddy's songs and the "Banks of the Ohio" and "Recuerdos de la Alhambra" and "Smile" and Stephen Foster and Boudleaux Bryant and the Beatles and "Freight Train," one long sparkling stream of music, as men in plaid pants hit their long, high-approach shots in a green paradise.

He said: "I enjoy the fruits of my efforts, but I have never felt comfortable promoting myself. The condition is worsening now that I am on the back nine. My passion for the guitar and for fame is slowly dying and it makes me sad. I never thought my love for the guitar would fade. There are a lot of reasons; as we get older the high frequencies go, music doesn't sound so good. And for some damn reason after hearing so many great players, I lose the competitive desire. Here I am baring my soul. That's good, though, isn't it? I'm not a Catholic, but I love that facet of their religion."

Chet was curious and thoughtful about religion, though he was dubious about shysters and TV evangelists. He said, "I am seventy and still don't know anything about life, what universal entity designed the body I live in or what will come after I am gone. I figure there will be eternity and nothing much else. Like pulling a finger out of water. If it as the Baptists claim, I think I would tire of streets of gold and would want to see brick houses. I believe that when I die I'll probably go to Minnesota. The last time I was up there, it was freezing and I remember smiling and my upper lip went up and didn't come back down."

God looks on the heart and is a God of mercy and loving kindness beyond our comprehension, and in that faith let us commend his spirit to the Everlasting, may the angels bear him up, and may eternal light shine upon him, and may he run into a lot of his old friends, and if he should wind up in Minnesota, we will do our best to take care of him until the rest of you come along.

Chapter 16

Apocalypse at High Noon

Why do some artists and their songs last until the end of time, while others are lost forever in the infinite ozone of too-far-gone, too-little-remembered?

Why is Johnny Cash successful today—far beyond other Johnny-Come-Lately performers who barely survived yesterday?

Will both Tracy Byrd and Tracy Lawrence be in favor tomorrow? Will both Ty Herndon and Ty England emerge from the gigantic shakedown caused by a plethora of competent acts colliding at the same time, like the break at a pool table when very few fortunate balls hit the pocket while the eight-ball remains omnipresent as a grim reminder of a dark fate?

How about Mark Chesnutt and Mark Collie? Is there room for both John Berry and John Michael Montgomery during this stressful sorting-out process? And Lorrie Morgan and Lari White? Brooks & Dunn and Montgomery/Gentry? Somebody's got to go. Something's got to give.

There's not enough room for all on the country radio station play lists, the trade magazine charts and the CD bins at record outlets.

The emerging stars who sear straight into the souls of fans possess the staying power to survive the upcoming artist Armageddon. Their hard-earned years, yearnings, dramas and dreams will catapult them into the high country of country music's class acts of the future.

Shania Twain, Faith Hill, the Dixie Chicks, Tim McGraw and fresh new faces will become the spokespersons of the new generation in country music, taking the torch from Garth Brooks, who raised the bar for them. They reach the masses and speak in a musical voice that rises above the cacophony of supposedly civilized living, circa 2003 and beyond. With the 20th Century in its rear view mirror, Planet Earth spins into a brave new world of high-tech progress and low-tech terrorism. The resurgence of patriotism, pride and cocky combativeness awakened on the dark day of September 11, 2001, changed the focus of Americans back to the roots of this country. Those rural roots reach deep, firmly embedded in the meaning and message of country music.

Some veterans and a handful of newcomers will survive the talent glut as the creators of the past, present and future engage in a velvet-gloved fight for critical radio and TV airplay, record sales, concert crowds and fan approval. The ship will sail stormy waters, but the best and brightest will discover that there's safe anchorage and an appreciative audience at home port.

Poets and Pickers

Songwriting philosophers such as Merle Haggard, Hank Williams and Roger Miller have chronicled the diverse and elusive pathways to happiness while lamenting their time wasted wandering the side streets of despair and failure.

"If we make it through December everything is going to be all right I know," Merle Haggard sings in a heart-breaking tone, exposing his hidden but honest belief that a laid-off worker and his stressed-out family can't make it through what he describes as "the coldest time of winter...I shiver when I see the falling snow." Unfortunately, there are a few million jobless citizens of this country who can relate to Haggard's woes related in "If We Make It Through December."

These artists spin haunting emotions into vivid every-day reality, enhancing country music's mainline connection to the common man and woman. Some songs are so powerful they become mini-anthems of our culture. Prime examples are Haggard's "Okie from Muskogee" and the late Johnny Paycheck's in-your-face performance of the David Allan Coe boss-busting classic, "Take This Job and Shove It."

Hank Williams wrote and sang lonely lyrics of love lost and heartache gained. "I'm So Lonesome I Could Cry" resonates with some of the most poetic imagery that has graced any genre of music, typified by the brilliant lyric, "The silence of a falling star lights up a purple sky." Only a genius at the top of his trade could conjure up the concept of silence lighting up anything, much less a purple sky. But none of Williams's dirges traversed a darker, more foreboding, pathway than "I'll Never Get Out of this World Alive." The mournful prophetic ballad topped the charts on the month that the 29-year-old falling star died of an excess of living. The title of Hank's farewell message roared into reality on January 1, 1953.

On the domestic front, Roger Miller, telling the sad tale of "Husbands and Wives," carved a poignant dissection of his marriage as it detoured into divorce. To a very simple melody Miller overlaid the overpowering words: "It's my belief pride is the chief cause in the decline in the number of husbands and wives." Ernest Hemingway couldn't have stated it better or more succinctly.

The Highwaymen Hit the Road

Four men who typify this breed of song-slingers, especially when they combined forces as the Highwaymen, helped shape the face and destiny of country music. Johnny Cash, Willie Nelson and the late, lamented Waylon Jennings all secured their sometimes treacherous passage into the Country Music Hall of Fame as individuals. Only Kris Kristofferson has yet to join his Highwaymen cohorts in the Hall of Fame, but his time will come. All four veterans achieved success in music and movies, but they relished sublimating personal show business accomplishments into the comfortable anonymity of making music as a group.

"I don't know of any other four spoiled old boys who are used to having it their own way who could do this," Jennings once told me. "We don't try to change one another that much. We can argue and call each other sonofabitches and still be all right because we respect each other and enjoy being around each other."

Johnny Cash totaled how many years of touring and friendship the foursome had accumulated and contributed

Gerry Wood introduces his Billboard *staffers to Kris Kristofferson. Left to right: Jo Walker-Meador (executive director of the Country Music Association), Kristofferson, Wood, Pat Halper and Sally Hinkle.*
(Photo courtesy of Gerry Wood)

this amount: "There's 137 years of road work up there on stage and 120 years of friendship."

The camaraderie was both offstage and on. Kristofferson, one of the all-time great songwriters, has never been known for his melodic tones or golden pipes. His raspy voice grovels from a growl to a grunt as it desperately seeks the proper key. Only his potent, penetrating lyrics save the day.

One night in the middle of a Highwaymen concert tour, an ill Kristofferson took the stage for his set and warned Willie Nelson, "I don't know if I can sing or not—I've got laryngitis."

Willie cast a long, quizzical glance at his buddy and asked a simple question. "How can you tell?"

That's what friends can say to each other. And that's why the Highwaymen had as much fun performing together as their fans had in watching four spectacular talents morph into a new energy and new voice. Icons on parade.

Sadly, Waylon Jennings died in 2002 at the age of 64 after a long battle with diabetes and its complications. He left a major mark on a country music industry that often resisted his stubborn, but correct, insistence to do things his way. The right way. The Waylon way. This Highwayman took the right road.

The George and Tammy Show, Part Two

Country music in the 1990s celebrated déjà vu moments with the reemergence of duet partners George Jones and Tammy Wynette, America's chart-topping fun couple from two decades earlier. Once husband and wife, they were married to others as they joined forces again for a new album and concert tour.

"He's my friend and I'm his friend," Tammy explained the changing state of their once contentious marital and martial relationship that supplied the tabloid publications with spicy fodder for years.

A respect for each other's soulful singing finally transformed the duo into a comfortable friendship and a chance to make magic again. "When I first heard Tammy on record, I thought she was about the finest gal singer to come along in many, many years," Jones praised during a Nashville video shoot with Wynette. "After all this time, I still feel the same way about her."

Before and after their initial award-winning duet popularity, Jones and Wynette took their solo careers to the top. Fans and critics alike frequently cite the George Jones tearjerker "He Stopped Loving Her Today" as the best song in country music history. And Wynette's former No. 1 hit "Stand By Your Man" regained its signature song status when Hillary Clinton mocked its message during a network television interview. Ironically, the First Lady at that moment was standing by her own man as President Bill Clinton battled the impeachment fallout during the Monica Lewinsky scandal.

Born Virginia Wynette Pugh, the frail and often hospitalized Tammy died at age 55 on April 6, 1998. Her memorial service took place at Nashville's historic Ryman Auditorium, a building where her voice, filled with heartache and hurt, ricocheted off the hallowed brick walls during Grand Ole Opry appearances. Among the stars, family and fans packing the Ryman to the rafters, George Jones, on the front row, was one of the most distraught.

For George Jones and for country music, déjà vu had just died.

Chapter 17

The Night I Slept with Elvis

The Whirl According to Merle

There's no better storyteller in the history of country music than Merle Kilgore, whose multi-faceted creative career includes the triple threat categories of songwriter, singer and actor. Kilgore's show business life has been attached to the name of Hank Williams—both Hank Sr. and Hank Jr. He started in Shreveport, Louisiana, at the tender age of 14 by carrying Hank Williams Sr.'s guitar, and now he manages Hank Williams Jr.

In 1954, while still a teenager, he wrote "More and More," a million-seller for Webb Pierce. After becoming an artist on *Louisiana Hayride*, the famous talent-launching show out of Shreveport, he wrote the mega-selling "Wolverton Mountain," that sent Claude King to the top of the charts. Then, co-writing with June Carter Cash, came a Johnny Cash signature song, "Ring of Fire." As an entertainer, appropriately dubbed the "Boogie King," he hit the

Merle Kilgore and Elvis.
(Photo courtesy of Merle Kilgore)

charts with several songs. His favorite remains "Mr. Garfield," recorded with a little help from his friends Hank Williams Jr. and Johnny Cash.

On the silver screen, this man—giant in stature and congeniality—appeared in such Hollywood hits as *Coal Miner's Daughter* and Robert Altman's critically acclaimed *Nashville*. More recently, Kilgore acted in the ultimate typecast role. He played himself in the life story of Hank Williams Jr., *Living Proof.*

But let's return to Merle Kilgore, storyteller. From Hank Sr. to Hank Jr., from the early days of the rise of country music to its current comfy position as a major player in American musical genres, he has been there, done that, and still has a lot to do. But country music executives and stars alike just want to get Merle talking about his travels.

Some of the stars talked to spirits, reports Kilgore, who describes a tour with Johnny Cash and an unusual stop along a rural road when they were driving to an appearance. Cash slammed on the brakes when he spotted a cow in a pasture. Pointing to the bovine, Cash exclaimed, "That's Johnny Horton!"

Merle has pretty much seen it all.

In the mid-1950s, Kilgore toured with an unknown struggling singer named Elvis Presley who would later become the biggest name in show business and a member of both the Country Music Hall of Fame and the Rock and Roll Hall of Fame. Merle recalls some memorable stories about traveling with the fast-rising, hip-shaking, world-changing performer. Here are some of those tales in the words of Merle Kilgore.

Life on a Landfill

My agent ran the artist service bureau of the *Louisiana Hayride* radio show in Shreveport when Elvis Presley signed up with the show. They told my agent that a good, lively act was needed to open for Elvis, and my agent told the *Hayride* people, "I know just the man." Then he came to me and said, "You're going to work with Elvis Presley."

"Oh, yeah!" I said. I had met Elvis at the *Hayride* and liked him as a performer and as a person. "Oh, yeah!"

The first thing Elvis said to me when we met was, "Merle Kilgore—you worked with Hank Williams."

"Yeah, I did."

"And you wrote 'More and More' that Webb Pierce song."

Elvis knew about my first hit as a songwriter.

"Listen, man," Elvis said, "ah, do you know Tibby Edwards?"

"He's my roommate. And not only that, we share dressing rooms together."

"Could I meet him?" Elvis asked.

"Come with me right now, Elvis. Don't you want to see a dressing room?"

"No, I really want to meet Tibby Edwards."

Tibby was a short, cute-looking Cajun musician on Mercury Records—a little-bitty wonderful guy. I loved him and he sang good. I went to the dressing room where Tibby had his Nudie Cohn suits hanging up.

"Hey, Tibby, put on your pants. Elvis Presley wants to meet you."

"Who's that?" Tibby asked.

"You know, the new guy. You know, 'That's All Right, Mama.'"

"Oh, yeah. Okay."

Elvis wasn't that well known and Tibby stayed on tour all the time, so that's why he didn't know about Elvis. Tibby put on his clothes and I introduced him to Elvis.

"Oh, man, that's a beautiful suit," Elvis said, admiring Nudie's artistic handiwork. "It's full of rhinestones." Elvis turned to me and said, "Hey, Merle, I *love* that art. That's all right, Mama!"

Elvis ended up using Tibby on a lot of his shows. He loved him, too.

Tibby called me a few years ago.

"Merle," he said, "thanks to you, reporters are starting to look me up, and they found me. All my life, I work construction and nobody ever believes I knew Elvis Presley. Somebody brought me a picture of Elvis and me. Man, I'm getting famous again!"

"What are you doing these days, Tibby?"

"I got me a trailer on a landfill here."

"On a *landfill?* I don't believe I'd say that to the press."

"It's a *new* trailer," he advised me, proudly.

Elvis Presley, Shoe Painter

When rock 'n' roll arrived, country music died. The first records that Elvis released started hitting the country charts before he ever made the pop and rock charts. He became more and more popular on the *Louisiana Hayride*, where the crowds went wild for him. As he toured in the South with other country performers, Elvis would pack them in, and the fans would sit through all the hillbilly music just to hear Elvis.

When Elvis left country music and became the number-one star of the new rock 'n' roll music, it killed country music at the time. It was slim pickings. But back at the beginning of his country career, Elvis was different from other performers, both onstage and off.

That day I met him, the first thing I noticed was that he was wearing a pink jacket and black pants. He wore black and white shoes and had painted the tops of them pink to match the jacket.

It was a lousy paint job. I looked down at his shoes, saw that paint job and said, "Oh, a home job."

"Yeah, Merle, I painted them," Elvis answered, impressed by his creative expertise with pink paint and a pair of shoes.

Bonded by a Mother's Name

The very first day we met, Elvis and I were driving down the road and he looked at me real funny.

"Man, I don't know how to say this," Elvis said.

"What is it?" I wondered. "Is it my hair? Is my bald spot showing?" I had a little bald spot then, and I thought I was covering it up real good.

"No," he answered, and then paused. "You'll think I'm crazy, man, but something was asking me to ask you what's your mama's name."

"My mama? My mama is named Gladys."

"Mine is too!" Elvis said, smiling.

"No kidding."

"Yeah, I ain't never met nobody who had a mama named Gladys."

"Me neither."

And he booked me on some of his shows. I opened for Elvis on the road for three shows in 1954 and 1955. He loved me because my mama was named Gladys.

Elvis Strikes Out

One day on a tour Elvis and I were in Texarkana, Arkansas, driving in Elvis's Cosmopolitan Lincoln that his manager Bob Neal had gotten him. It was his first new car and had 5,000 miles on it. Elvis loved it and wouldn't let anybody smoke in it. You had to get outside to smoke.

"Merle, I have found us two beautiful women," Elvis told me. He was real excited.

"Alright!" I got excited, too.

"They're beauticians," he explained. "They live together."

I felt fortunate because usually one's pretty and the other one is ugly. And I know which one I would have gotten if that was the case with me and Elvis.

"Man, we're in luck," Elvis said.

Elvis told his musicians, Scotty Moore and Bill Black, to go on in their car to Shreveport. We would stay and get a little motel room and return to Shreveport later.

The first thing we did after picking up the girls was to go out to this old-timey drive-in restaurant. Boy! I was so cool driving around in the back seat of that car, getting acquainted with my new girlfriend. They were so happy to be with Elvis. He had just stolen the show at Texarkana's little city auditorium, and had just jammed the fans in.

At the restaurant, Elvis wanted hamburgers for everyone. He loved hamburgers. The girls really didn't want hamburgers. Elvis got kind of mad.

"You don't want a hamburger? These are real good. I've eaten here before."

Elvis ordered a hamburger with double onions, and the same thing for me. The girls settled for grilled cheese sandwiches.

It was a great hamburger, and I praised his hamburger knowledge.

After finishing our food, we went to their house. Elvis said to me, "Look. Here's the deal. They have one room that they rent and they both sleep in the same bed. I'll go in with my girl first. You get acquainted with yours in the back seat. Then we'll come out and sit in the car while y'all are inside."

So when Elvis and his girl left for the bedroom, I was in the back seat of that big Lincoln, putting on the charm and fogging up the windows. A short time later we heard a loud knock on the window. We both thought it was the cops, and we jumped about twenty feet.

I rolled down the window and found that it was Elvis knocking.

Elvis told the girl that her friend asked for her inside and Elvis told me, "You might as well get up in the front seat."

"What? What happened Elvis?"

"Man, I don't know. I'm telling you we got on the bed and just started kissing, and she told me, 'Look, this is not going to work out. I can feel it. Why don't you go get my girlfriend, and you and your friend better leave. I really enjoyed meeting you, but I can tell this is not going to work.'"

We left the beauticians and drove to that little motel. Our room didn't even have linoleum on the floor. It cost us five dollars for one night. And it didn't even have a phone.

You had to go out to the parking lot to call, and it was real cold outside.

In those days it was proper to share a bed together to save money so you wouldn't have to pay extra. All the musicians on the road always did that. So we both had to sleep in the same bed.

I got in bed, but Elvis kept pacing that rickety, creaky floor. There was no way I could sleep.

"Come on in bed, man," I told him

"I'm telling you, I don't understand it," Elvis said as he stomped across the floor. "I've been re-living this whole thing in my mind. What do you think went wrong between me and that girl?"

"I know *exactly* what went wrong, Elvis." Recalling that my hamburger came with a huge double order of onions, I asked him, "Did you order double onions on your hamburger?"

"Yeah. For me and you."

"Onions, man!" I told him. "That turned her off. When she said that this wasn't going to work out, it was the onions."

Now Elvis understood that his onion breath had messed up his plans for the bedroom. "She'll be sorry one day," he promised.

"She will," I reassured him. "And nobody will believe her!"

Elvis finally got to laughing and got in bed. He went to sleep just like that—snoring in no time at all.

Don't you know that woman has thought about that a million times after Elvis became so famous?

I can see her telling people later that she kicked Elvis Presley out of her bed.

She kicked Elvis out of her bed? Sure. Nobody's going to buy that story.

Chapter 18

Melodies in the Mountains with Michael Martin Murphey

Country and **Real** *Western Music*

The sun slides behind the mountains, crimson tentacles of fiery neon rays fleck the snow-laced peaks and cascade down to the tree lines, fingering deeper until succumbing to the shadows in the sheltered valleys.

So pure and sweet, the pine-scented air could be sold as candy if it could be crystallized. The trees whisper their sweet mountain song as the wind carries chill and the foreboding weathervane hints of a harsh winter ahead.

Closer to the valley, more music joins the serenade of the pines. Mandolin and guitars, then the sound of Native American drums, a touch of Tejano, mournful country songs and plaintive cowboy ballads that would encourage even a New Yorker to saddle up and ride. "Home on the Range," sounds just as at-home up here in the Colorado Rockies as it did back home on the range.

Michael Martin Murphey—he's country and real *western.*
(Photo courtesy of Gerry Wood)

The melodies rise from a stage at the base of Copper Mountain, where 14,000 music lovers turn the gentle green slope into a patchwork of colors with their western garb, lawn chairs and blankets. Performing is the maestro of cowboy and mountain music, Michael Martin Murphey, the former Texas pop star who enjoyed such major hits as "Wildfire" and "Geronimo's Cadillac."

Every bit as dapper and dashing as his idol Buffalo Bill Cody, Murphey has the crowd in his hands with one song after another denoting his decades as one of America's most gifted entertainers. Ballads from his pop past fling a nostalgic ring, along with number one country chart toppers such as "What's Forever For" and "A Long Line of Love," and his latest, and enduring, passion—songs of the American West.

The voice is soft and longing, a subtle urge to return to a simpler world, or at least recreate it with precision and perfection. The spirit is exalted and soaring. The handsome man with sweetness in his face and voice has the mountains at his command as the ballads sweep through the enchanted audience and filter up the hills on their way to the heavens.

"Red River Valley." "Tumbling Tumbleweeds." "Cool Water." "Back in the Saddle Again." And the show-closing finale, "Happy Trails," written by Dale Evans and made famous by her husband Roy Rogers, the western movie and TV hero and member of the Country Music Hall of Fame. Backed by the Colorado Springs Symphony Orchestra conducted by Christopher Wilkins, whose cowboy hat is as notable as his baton, the classical-cowboy combination proves breathtaking.

A slight diversion here—there is country music and there is western music. They are two separate entities, though joined at the hip and, somewhat, at the head. Hank Williams is country music, not western. Roy Rogers is western

Michael Martin Murphey backstage at WestFest
with Carol Shaughnessy and Gerry Wood.
(Photo courtesy of Gerry Wood)

music, not country. Merle Haggard is country music, not western. Don Edwards is western music, not country. Michael Martin Murphey *was* country and is *now* western. Got it? Me neither. But just remember that they are two different forms of one massive genre of music that fall under one category when convenient.

All that is great about country music and western music and other modes of music and creative expression—from arts and crafts to food—comes alive at Murphey's WestFest in Colorado. Through the years the artists have included unknowns that soon became knowns: Clint Black, Rick

Trevino, Darryl Worley, Dwight Yoakam, k.d. lang, the Dixie Chicks. And knowns that became greater-knowns: Vince Gill, Tracy Lawrence, Dan Seals, Suzy Bogguss, Robert Earl Keen, Lonestar, Mary Chapin Carpenter, Jerry Jeff Walker, Kelly Willis, Crystal Gayle, Hal Ketchum, Ronnie Milsap, Guy Clark, Merle Haggard and Native Americans such as the Morning Star Dancers, medicine man Bearheart, Bill Miller and Robert Mirabal.

Asleep at the Wheel woke up the wilderness with western swing that motivated the late Bob Wills into a two-stepping frenzy somewhere upstairs, while Wills's old band, the Texas Playboys, continued to entertain WestFest fans. Cowboy crooners like Don Edwards and Sons of the San Joaquin took the stage bracketed by Tejano talents Tish Hinojosa and La Diferenzia. Delightfully funny and philosophic cowboy poets bring their rhymes and reasons down to earth in stories and song as the fans enjoy Baxter Black and Waddie Mitchell. The sartorially splendid Riders in the Sky, wearing western duds to die for, gain repeated WestFest visits, their shows laced with laughter, keen witticisms and winsome vocal harmonies.

The Unbroken Circle

The eclectic elements that elevate WestFest above and beyond other festivals merge into their own life force during this showcase that wanders from western swing to southwestern song, from mountain men to city dwellers, from cowboys to Indians. The foray into the art, music, lifestyle and mindset of the great American West fuses generations, creeds and cultures into an oval rainbow that forgives the past, survives the present and promises hope for the future.

But more than any other factor, the event derives its ultimate energy and spirit from Native Americans.

"I've always been drawn to the Indian people because they really know this land," Murphey told me during a WestFest held in Vail, Colorado.

"The rest of us are just immigrants here. They are the real spiritual soul of WestFest. Indian people developed a cosmology, a sense of the whole universe that influences us still today."

Murphey maintains that the Indians taught the less educated inhabitants of the globe about the first ecology, along with the first balance in nature, the first sense of man blending in to what God offers.

"They taught that we're in a circle, that man isn't at the top of the heap like we were taught. The spirit of WestFest is that circle. Michael Martin Murphey is not at the top and everybody who has a little booth here is not at the bottom. I'm just in the circle with everybody else, and the circle is never ending."

On stage, Michael performs a stunning guitar solo version of "Wildfire," gazing beyond the first-row fans, his distant eyes searching for the mountain ridge, losing himself in the golden setting circle of the sun. As his mother and father proudly watch from side stage, Michael becomes a creative channel, the music surging down skyward through his soul and out into the audience—from sun to son to sun.

The circle not only was unbroken. It was expanding.

The Best Fest of All

Murphey launched his Colorado WestFests in the mid-1980s, and he has spun off traveling versions into other western locales. Somehow, though, the Colorado Rockies cuddle and nurture this magical merger of music and muse with more warmth and magnetism than any other spot on earth. The horror of September 11, 2001 brings even more relevance and importance to Murphey's mission of getting one neighbor to talk to another, one race to sit down and dine with another, one culture to sing with another, one country to reach out and touch spirits with another, one generation to form a bond with past generations while making this planet a better place to live for the children and grandchildren who endure these troubled times of worry and war.

"You're able to forget about time out here at WestFest," Suzy Bogguss revealed after performing and roaming the Indian and Mountain Man villages and southwestern arts and crafts exhibits. "There's a homecoming feel to it, even if you're not from the West—it's a special mindset. It clears everything from your mind except a time when things were a lot simpler and, perhaps, a lot better."

Offstage and on, a gentleness turns frenzy to fun, manic to magic, turmoil to peace. The sounds of laughter ring out from the audience as Pam Tillis, who's part Native American, jokingly tells the crowd, "My Indian name is Running Mascara." Members of the hit-making group Lonestar sit down on hay bales and munch away on an authentic chuck wagon meal cooked in old iron kettles. Ranger Doug Green of the Riders in the Sky, always on the prowl for another addition to his extensive western wardrobe, offers an important piece of purchasing advice. "Put a portion of your paycheck away," he told me, "because this is going to cost you dearly."

However, Hal Ketchum, fresh off the stage and watching a group of trail riders head up a mountain pass, enjoyed a WestFest specialty that cost nothing at all. "This place makes me feel even stronger spiritually," Ketchum noted as he and his wife Gina marveled at the buffalo-hide bonnet cases in the style of those once used by Plains Indians.

While some country singers decline in popularity and watch their careers go South, Michael Martin Murphey saw his career go West. And he's never regretted it.

"I always envisioned WestFest as a dialogue, a teaching experience and a seminar," explains Michael who also has taught university courses in American West cultural studies. He follows the wisdom of Walt Disney, quoting the movie and theme park king as saying, "In every great piece of entertainment there's a little education, and in every piece of education there should be a little entertainment."

What Goes Around Comes Around

WestFest is winding down for another year. The last night—many head for the bar at the resort. And the old Wild West surges to life again. Mountain men clad in scruffy fur. Western women dressed to the nines in elaborate antique finery adorned with brooches and jewelry from past centuries that live anew. Cowboys with ever-present ten-gallon hats and massive belt buckles demonstrate their undying allegiance to the once-dying western way while cowboy poets tweak their waxed-down handlebar moustaches. Country music fans wearing jeans, cowboy boots and western shirts belly up to the bar, elbow to elbow with Native

Americans in their colorful feathered garb. It's America's finest fashion statement, and it's heartwarming to watch.

They raise toasts to each other. A liquid crossing of man-made, mandated borders into uncharted cultural communities. They don't totally understand each other—the gulfs are great and have been stretched thin with words and warring through the years. But now it comes together through the playful shouts and laughter and listening to strangers who become friends. All because of music, Michael's message and the camaraderie it imparts on these people in the boisterous Colorado mountainside watering hole.

A Native American, head bearing a feathered halo, quotes Chief Seattle to an enchanted audience of cowpokes, miners, mountain men, country singers and city slickers: "How can you buy the sky? How can you own the rain and the wind? My mother told me, 'Every part of this earth is sacred to my people. Every pine needle, every sandy shore, all are holy in the memory of our people.'"

The Indian's deep and resonant voice, rising like the spoken wisdom of a prophet, begins to conquer and quiet the din of the bar dwellers. Even the clink of glasses and the incessant chatter cease completely. Realizing that he now holds the attention of the entire establishment, a look of peace crosses the Indian's face, rutted deep as a dark brown western trail burrowing through pines and along the banks of tiny streams that grow to raging rivers. As the revelers wait for more words from the past that can profit the future, he continues:

"Grandfather said to me, 'The air is precious and it shows its spirit with all of the life it supports. The wind that gave me my first breath also receives my last sigh.'"

The room becomes so quiet that a breeze through his majestic headdress of feathers could have been heard.

"This we know," the sage speaks. "All things are connected like the blood that unites us. We did not weave the web of life; we are merely a strand in it. Whatever we do to the web we do to ourselves. We love this earth as a newborn loves its mother's heartbeat. Preserve the land, the air and the rivers for your children's children and love it as we have loved it."

The message melts into the minds of his listeners, some who are wiping away tears, and the Native American chief sits down, sinking deep into his chair, looking tired and triumphant, enchanted and exhausted, at the same time. In honor of this descendant of our nation's founding tribes, and in tribute to Chief Seattle, glasses are raised high and clinked together, a crystal wind chime that echoes far beyond the Rockies. Handshakes and gentle pats on the old Indian's back follow as a line forms before him to express appreciation for this timeless dialogue of wisdom and strength, and his philosophy on how to prevail.

And, after an appropriate pause, the noise slowly returns to the bar, this time softer and a little more muted.

Country music and all its champions, western music and all its heroes, could never provide a more meaningful discourse than the soulful encounters that graced this tavern on this evening. The eternal words of Chief Seattle settled over the final night of WestFest with the serenity of peace in the valley and the warmth of a snug blanket over the spirits of the past and all those fortunate enough to be living now, blessed with the privilege and opportunity to carry on the tradition of seeking a better world for all mankind in the future.